Winging it

Birding for low-flyers

Andrew Fallan

Brambleby Books

Winging it – Birding for low-flyers
©Andrew Fallan 2011

ISBN 978-0-9553928-5-6

Published 2011 by
Brambleby Books Ltd.
www.bramblebybooks.co.uk

Cover design by Tanya Warren, Creatix
Printed for Brambleby Books by
Berforts Print, U.K., on PEFC certified paper.

Dedicated to Kasia and Jesse –
young nature lovers in-the-making

Behold the fowls of the air: for they sow not, neither do they reap, nor gather into barns…
Matthew 6: 26, KJV

I went to the woods because I wished to live deliberately, to front only the essential facts of life, and see if I could not learn what it had to teach, and not, when I came to die, discover that I had not lived.
Henry David Thoreau (1817-62)

Contents

8

About the Author

Andrew Fallan grew up in south-east Essex in the 1970s and early 80s. As a young boy a memorable close encounter with a Kestrel sparked a passion for birds and the natural world, which would be sustained by regular birding adventures with his older brother.

Although his interest in birds waned with the onset of his teenage years, a life-changing trip to the rugged and beautiful Isle of Skye, in Scotland, fostered a keen interest in hillwalking and climbing, which was pursued with the same enthusiasm that was once reserved for chasing after birds.

In his early 30s, Andrew and his brother returned once more to Minsmere, the RSPB's flagship reserve on the Suffolk coast, for a day's birding – just for 'old times' sake'. This would eventually lead to a resurgence of the birding bug that was first roused by an unsuspecting Kestrel all those years before. Along the way Andrew also met that 'special lady', with whom he continued to pursue his rekindled passion for birding and wildlife, and with whom he currently lives in Southend-on-Sea, in Essex. They also live with a very special cat named Colin, who unfortunately does not share their interest in birding.

Foreword by Chris Packham

The first bird I ever identified was a summer plumage male Baltimore Oriole. Its bright yellow plumage reflected off the water beneath the rock on which it was perched just beneath a mill pool on the river Itchen in Hampshire and matched identically the illustration in my brand-new field guide – in the rarities section. I was so excited about my 'discovery' that I raced home and announced the 'Ornithological Event of the Century' to my father. He put down his newspaper, perused the page thrust before him, flicked through a few more, raised his eyebrows and uttered two deadpan words . . . grey and wagtail. You don't forget that much embarrassment, you learn from it, and if you are a real naturalist you keep learning from it all your life.

Sometimes interviewers ask me what is my most important skill. The answer is very simple, never being afraid to say I don't know. Know-it-alls don't exist, big headed idiots do, but they always get found out. I'd like to say that this species of naturalist or birder was a rarity but unfortunately they seem to be hanging on despite the massive and welcome surge of interest in wildlife over the last 25 years or so. Thinking back, there used to be one in every hide I visited as a schoolboy beginner, so things have improved and more people seem to realise that honesty is the best policy.

That's why I like Andrew's book: it's totally honest and he is even frank in his opinions about ringing. I don't agree with him about this one bit but I certainly respect him for not sitting on the fence. I do definitely concur with his thoughts on a proportion of the twitching fraternity though. They actually put me off birding in the UK for a while in the same fashion as football thuggery put me off going to see the beautiful game. But anyway I no longer even count them as birders, merely a sad group of feather-grabbing zombies who contribute nothing to the proper interest that most of us have. Not that they are all bad of course.

I hope that you also enjoy his enthusiastic romps and respond through recognition to his highs and lows, and you will be reassured that he, indeed we, are out there wearing the friendly face of down to earth good ol' honest birding.

Chris Packham

PS I did eventually see a Baltimore Oriole, in the 90s, in the USA. It wasn't as good as that Grey Wagtail though!

Acknowledgements

I would like to thank all at Brambleby Books, particularly Nicola Loxdale for her unfailing patience, advice and support; Chris Packham and his managing agent, David Foster, for the foreword; my wife, Amanda (aka Panda), for her continued encouragement and support, and for always believing in the book; my brother Pete, for helping to fill the gaps in my memory concerning our past birding adventures; and last but definitely not least, my ever-obliging parents, for providing a first class – and free – taxi service in my early birding years!

It started with a Kestrel...

Many birders can undoubtedly trace their interest in birds to a specific event or sighting, usually occurring in childhood, or at least identify a specific time that their interest in birds was first roused. For example, in *Birders – Tales of a Tribe*, Mark Cocker (2001) describes how, as an eight-year-old looking around in the attic of his dad's shop, he was startled by a flurry of activity as some pigeons hurriedly made off through a hole in the roof. In a cavity between some broken floorboards, he found several pigeons' nests, complete with clutches of pure white eggs. In his childhood naivety, Cocker then set about 'rescuing' the eggs, and, once he had placed them in the 'safety' of an old shoebox, they became a "childhood treasure, to be opened and examined after school". He identified this event as being "the very earliest origins, the primeval beginnings, the *Archaeopteryx* in my personal story as a birder."

My own personal *Archaeopteryx* occurred when I was older than eight – probably more like eleven or twelve years old. The nature of such childhood memories is that the mind tends only to retain certain key images and feelings, with the finer details and context being somewhat 'fuzzy around the edges'. However, I do vividly recall a flurry of excitement when my brother Pete and I saw a Kestrel perched close-by on the roof of a low building at the Shell Club – a private members' club for the employees of the nearby Shell oil refinery near where we lived in Corringham, Essex. After allowing us a brief glimpse into its private world, the Kestrel gracefully lifted off into the air and flew effortlessly away – perhaps to delight some other fortunate soul, to be ignored, or to seek solitude altogether from prying eyes. I seem to recall that this bird also rather obligingly left us a feather, as if in an attempt to compensate for its swift departure, or maybe in deference to the interest it had inspired. This feather would have been retrieved eagerly and kept as a childhood treasure, much like Mark Cocker's pigeons' eggs.

I'm not sure how we knew this bird was a Kestrel, as we would not have been in possession of any field guides, and neither of us had any particular knowledge of birds. In the absence of any concrete memory, logic informs me that the most likely explanation is that a mutual friend alerted us to its presence.

This experience had a definite impact upon me, and I clearly remember feeling that we had seen something special, and something that very few people are privileged to see, at least at such close quarters. It was not that I assumed Kestrels to be especially rare, but more a feeling that we had happened upon a beautiful, spectacular and impressive bird, and been permitted a fleeting but intimate glimpse into its own private world. The fact that it was a bird of prey is also surely of significance, as I'm certain that if we had seen a little brown warbler, even if it was an extremely rare one (not that we would have known anyway), we would likely not even have looked twice at it.

Surely many other birders – and also non-birders – will agree that there is something rather exciting and alluring about birds of prey. After all, there can be very few people who would not be impressed at the sight of a Peregrine in high-speed aerial pursuit after its quarry, or a Sparrowhawk dashing through the trees in an attempt to out-manoeuvre and snatch a small bird fleeing for its life. Although most of us recoil from the violence, brutality and death inherent in nature, there is surely something impressive and awe-inspiring about these winged killing machines, these perfectly adapted predators that patrol the skies, effortlessly wheeling, soaring and dashing at break-neck speed, like high-tech fighter jets tearing through the skies to wreak havoc and destruction. I still harbour a fascination with birds of prey, and among my most treasured birding memories are my sightings of these spectacular creatures: Red Kites wheeling over the wooded valleys of central Wales; Goshawks soaring menacingly over the Forest of Dean; White-tailed Eagles spreading their enormous wings against the majestic backdrop of the Isles of Skye and Mull; Montagu's Harriers performing a mid-air food pass over the nest in the arable fields of Norfolk; and a crazed Merlin, striking terror into a group of small birds freshly put to flight by a beautiful male Hen Harrier, marauding like a silver phantom across the winter wasteland of the Isle of Sheppey in north Kent. Perhaps my lifelong fascination with birds of prey can be traced back to this childhood encounter with a Kestrel. Or perhaps it is because birds of prey evoke in us a deep sense of awe for the impressive and spectacular in life, and bring into sharp contrast both the immediacy and the sleek and savage beauty of nature. Perhaps it is a combination of both of these factors.

I remember going back to the same spot shortly afterwards in an attempt to see the Kestrel again. In my ornithological innocence, I assumed it had a nest there, and that because I had seen it there once, chances were that I would see it again (I did not). However, perhaps my subsequent interest in birds and birding can be seen as an attempt to once again capture the thrill of this chance encounter, this fleeting glimpse of the special, the beautiful, the spectacular.

Birding for low-flyers

Perhaps the first popular book about birding was *Bill Oddie's Little Black Bird Book.* Please note that this book is about birding rather than about birds. There are many books – old and new, scientific and not-so-scientific, and of many different genres – that are about birds. However, *BOLBBB* (as it has been abbreviated) is the first popular book, at least that I'm aware of, that takes a long, hard and also very tongue-in-cheek and humorous look at birders themselves and what makes them tick. Oddie also goes to great lengths to explain what exactly a birder is, i.e. as opposed to an ornithologist, bird-spotter / bird-fancier, bird-watcher, twitcher or 'dude'. Since the publication of this book in 1980, birding has become ever more popular, moving further and further into mainstream popular culture. Birding has also become a highly mechanised pursuit, particularly with the recent advent of pagers, mobile phones and Internet communication, not to mention the massive advances in optical technology (more of which later). With birding in all its forms becoming ever more popular among a greater percentage of the population, there have been a number of books published in recent years which, following on from *BOLBBB*, analyse birders and the entire pursuit, lifestyle and subculture of birding.

Birding has also produced its own legends, celebrities and high-flyers. For example, there is the late Richard Richardson, who could be found holding court among eager young birders on the east bank at Cley, on the north Norfolk coast, and whose legend, it seems, was famed among the UK birding community. There is also the very much contemporary Lee G.R. Evans, who is undoubtedly the UK's most renowned twitcher, and quite possibly also the most obsessive. Then there are those names that seem to be synonymous with top-level birding, like Dick Filby, Steve Gantlett and Richard Millington, and doubtless many others of whom I've never even heard. There's also Bryan Bland – he of the long grey beard, who can be seen roaming around East Anglia (and no doubt further afield), decked out in a smock, sandals and shorts, even in subarctic conditions. And then there are those birders that everyone encounters, who we all look up to and envy. You know the ones I mean: the ones with top-level optics and top-level birding skills to match; the ones who can see a dot a mile away and tell you exactly what species it is, or, based on barely visible variations in plumage, or from the faintest of skulking calls, accurately separate species that, to the eyes and ears of us mere mortals, are identical. In short, these people are the kind of birders that we'd all like to be: good birders!

In identifying myself with the massed ranks of birding 'low-flyers' out there, what I am basically saying is that I cannot lay claim to any of the skills, abilities, achievements or reputations of some of the top names – past and present – within the birding community. I have never been so consumed by birds and birding that – like Dick Filby, Steve Gantlett and Richard Millington – I have made a career out of it, or simply indulged my passion without thought of pursuing a career or finding a partner. I have never chartered planes and chased after rarities at the drop of a hat, and I have most certainly never been – nor will I ever be – a highly acclaimed, almost mythical twitcher and top 'year lister', like Lee Evans is (I have never even kept a year list!). And I have never excavated a hole in my bedroom roof in order to add Ferruginous Duck to my garden bird list, like Bryan Bland has; actually, I'm more likely to win the lottery than see a Ferruginous Duck from my garden! I cannot even lay claim to being a highly skilled and knowledgeable birder, or an accomplished county bird recorder or local 'patch-watcher'. I can probably count the number of birds on both hands that I can accurately identify by their calls alone. I'm hopeless at identifying waders, immature gulls, and all but the more obvious 'little brown jobs'. And I'm lost without often detailed

17

reference to my trusted field guides. Apart from when I first started birding and was limited by the lack of a car, I have never faithfully watched my local patch, nor have I ever kept detailed notes and sketches of all my sightings. And the thought of doing counts of waders or gull roosts would very likely elicit in me the desire to wail and bash the floor with my fists, like a traumatised Basil Fawlty.

However, having said all that, I can't even claim to be a particularly bad birder. There are many birds that I *am* able to identify in an instant, and compared to someone who knows nothing about birds, I'm a veritable expert. I have also seen some fairly impressive birds in my time, including what I believe was only the second ever Little Whimbrel recorded in the UK. Neither can I claim to be a non-birder, who simply enjoys birds and is content with a yearly trip to Minsmere – the RSPB's flagship reserve on the Suffolk coast – to watch the Chaffinches as I enjoy cake and savour a pot of tea. No, I am definitely a birder. Not a particularly good one, nor an especially bad one – just a *very* ordinary and rather mediocre one. Who knows, maybe I'm just like you...

Boys, bikes and birds

As a young boy growing up in south Essex in the 70s and early 80s, I was as dependent upon my bike (sorry, 'push-bike' and 'bicycle' are far too formal) as most adults are upon their cars. My bike was an integral part of me, almost becoming an extra limb, and as an enthusiastic adolescent who had just been well and truly bitten by the birding bug, it was essential to my very existence.

My older brother and I, together with one or more fellow enthusiasts, would take off on our bikes to the local birding spots, with the proverbial wind in our hair and free from the constraints of school, parents and the rest of the human world. 'Birding spots' doesn't necessarily mean nice, attractive, well-managed nature reserves, or even places frequented by other birders. I simply mean places where there was some semblance of what could be referred to as 'countryside', and where there was the outside chance of clapping eyes on some half-decent birds – though what constitutes a 'half-decent bird' is, of course, entirely subjective.

Fobbing marshes

First and foremost among these birding spots was Fobbing marshes, a large area of rough grazing land adjacent to the oil refinery, along the banks of the Thames at Coryton in southeast Essex. I doubt whether this area of land was known as 'Fobbing marshes' by anyone other than us, or whether it even qualified as a marsh in terms of a wildlife habitat. However, the name seemed as appropriate as any other, overlooked as it was by the small village of Fobbing nestled atop a modest hill, and which served as our ever-present place of refuge after a cold and lonely walk to the ends of the earth beyond.

Although on a much less grandiose scale in terms of terrain,

Fobbing marshes are similar to the Isle of Sheppey in Kent: vast areas of tussocky grass, hardly any trees to speak of, endless ranks of cows, and a general sense of bleakness and desolation that makes one yearn for nice, attractive, well-managed nature reserves with visitor centres and cafés. Unlike the Isle of Sheppey, however, Fobbing marshes boast no RSPB reserve, National Nature Reserve (NNR) or raptor viewpoint. And in place of the spacious backdrop of the Medway and Thames estuaries, there is the unnatural blight of the vast oil refinery – ranks of enormous cylindrical storage tanks, a tangled labyrinthine network of hissing and steaming pipes, and the industrial chimneys, forever belching forth their murky vapour clouds. There is also the ever-present crackling hum of the overhead power cables, drawing one's attention upwards to the enormous metal pylons that, rather ironically, can almost go unnoticed if one does not have cause to look specifically in their direction.

Fobbing marshes is also the kind of place where, as well as having to run the gauntlet of aggressive and scary looking cattle, you could, after walking only a very short distance, become a foot taller due to the cattle-churned mud that seemed to become welded to your boots (we would chain our bikes to a stile on the footpath and then walk the mile or so out across the marshes). If you were unlucky enough to trip over, or if you became tired and gave in to the urge to have a quick sit down, you also risked the subsequent wrath of angry parents, who demanded to know why you had been trying to get as muddy as possible, as it wasn't *you* that had to do the washing; and why couldn't you be like other children whose idea of fun *wasn't* to head out into the middle of a muddy wasteland on a cold and wet afternoon. Our answer on this particular occasion was that we had been trying to find a Bittern that had apparently been reported in the area. Catching a glimpse of this rare and elusive bird would have more than made up for any amount of cold, rain, congealed mud or parental wrath. Did we see the Bittern? Did we hell!

I think the first bird we encountered on one of our many expeditions to Fobbing marshes was a Goldfinch. Strictly speaking, we saw this bird on the journey there rather than on the marshes themselves, though the sighting does stick in my mind for a number of reasons. Firstly, I'm pretty sure it was the first time I had seen this species, and I was mesmerised by how striking and beautiful its bold combination of colours was. Secondly, the bird was lying in the road, as dead as the parrot of Monty Python sketch fame. However, unlike the dead parrot, the Goldfinch's head had been neatly separated from the rest of its body, which was lying a few feet away in the road. This is an ex-Goldfinch! This Goldfinch has ceased to be! I'm guessing it had been the casualty of one of the many vehicles that thunder mercilessly along this road, including an endless procession of oil tankers. In retrospect, this unfortunate creature could not even be credited with providing me with a new bird or 'tick', as it has been made very clear, by none other than Bill Oddie in his *Little Black Bird Book*, that you most definitely cannot include dead birds. At the time, however, I was likely oblivious to such birding formalities. I'm sure it wouldn't have bothered me anyway, as I was too busy savouring this rare close-up glimpse of such a uniquely beautiful bird, not to mention mourning its rather ignoble passing.

The deceased Goldfinch may also have afforded my brother and me our first eager foray into the rather unpleasant habit of preserving and collecting birds' wings. The wings would be removed from the dead bird, mounted on a nice piece of wood (which I think we either purchased or begged from our school's woodwork department) and then covered in 'cling-film'. Macabre as this sounds to adult ears (including my own), at the time we were motivated by a simple desire to preserve, prolong and enjoy the beauty of the birds that we loved. We took no pleasure in dismembering our feathered friends, just in the enjoyment of the finished product. Thankfully, however, our interest in collecting bird wings soon fizzled out – maybe it was

21

the smell.

Fobbing marshes did, however, possess avian delights other than dead Goldfinches en-route. Not long after being mesmerised by the Kestrel at the Shell Club, I remember happening upon another of these birds on Fobbing marshes. What really sticks in my mind about this sighting is the naive thrill I felt. Because we had seen a single Kestrel on Fobbing marshes, I assumed that these birds must have been breeding there. I remember thinking that we had found an undiscovered haven for wildlife that the world needed to be informed of in order that it could be duly protected. I fantasised about my 15 minutes of fame. I would write to TV's *The Really Wild Show* to inform them of this wildlife oasis with its breeding Kestrels, and the land would thereby be purchased and turned into a nature reserve. (Who remembers *The Really Wild Show?* There was the one and only Chris Packham, now of BBC's *Spring-* and *Autumnwatch* fame, though then sporting a bleached Billy Idol style quiff; Michaela Strachan, a vision of loveliness for any self-respecting young boy with a passion for wildlife; and – last but not least – Terry Nutkins, with his rather bizarre combination of long hair and baldness.) Of course, the next few times I went to Fobbing marshes the Kestrel was nowhere to be seen and my interest, together with the thought of writing to *The Really Wild Show*, started to fade. However, another source of intense excitement around this time was our discovery – or so we thought – of an extremely rare bird breeding on the marshes.

On one of the many expeditions to what had undoubtedly become our local patch, as we were walking along the footpath close to where we had previously seen the Kestrel, we noticed some fairly large birds to our right. They were flying pretty close to the ground with lazy wing-beats, and gliding intermittently with their wings held in a shallow 'V'. To our almost uncontainable joy, we concluded that Marsh Harriers had taken up residence and started to breed on the marshes. Wow! Marsh

Harriers breeding on Fobbing marshes – discovered by us! Remember, this was in the early 80s, when these harriers were still extremely rare breeding birds, and long before the dramatic resurgence that this species has seen in recent years. Nowadays, if you go to the raptor viewpoint at Capel Fleet on the Isle of Sheppey, just across the Thames in Kent, you cannot move for wintering Marsh Harriers.

I'm unsure exactly why we identified these birds as Marsh Harriers, as we did not see any plumage details or specific diagnostic features, nor were we especially familiar with the 'jizz' of this species (the characteristic features of a bird's general appearance and behaviour, such that it is often possible to identify species on the basis of this alone, and without reference to specific diagnostic features such as plumage details). These birds were undoubtedly harriers (we had *some* birding knowledge even at this young age), though in all likelihood we made the assumption that, as they were harriers frequenting a marsh, they must be Marsh Harriers – at least we were logical. In our ever-present ornithological naivety, we also assumed that the presence of these birds indicated that they had taken up residence and were breeding on the marshes. I cannot recall exactly what time of year we saw these birds, but the likelihood is that they were in fact overwintering. It is therefore still entirely possible that they were indeed Marsh Harriers, though it is also just as likely that they were wintering Hen Harriers.

We once saw another 'star bird' on Fobbing marshes, though it was much further out than the harriers. One winter's day – likely both cold and miserable in equal measure – we were making our way along the footpath, which meandered among gangs of brooding cattle that would watch our every move, some half a mile or so from the safety of our chained-up bikes. To our left was a small, dreary river that moped – you could hardly say it flowed – all the way to the large tidal creek at the far side of the marsh, which thankfully marked the limits of our adventures. On a bad day such excursions could feel more like a forced march.

As would be expected of adolescent boys, our birding excursions were also motivated by the desire for exploration, adventure and good old-fashioned fun. On this particular day, the birds must have been somewhat thin on the ground, as our interests soon became focused upon a very large piece of polystyrene bobbing up and down in the murky river. As if it would be rude not to, we immediately tried to commandeer it as some kind of raft to take us to the other side. However, we soon discovered that the laws of physics were not on our side. Rather than risk a dunking, we abandoned the idea in favour of finding a narrower stretch of water and making a running jump for it. The laws of gravity were, however, still plotting our demise, and when our birding companion took the initial jump, only the top half of his body hit dry land, his lower legs getting drenched in the dirty water. This was the cause of much hilarity, and we laughed hysterically at his sodden misfortune (remember, he would have to walk the half mile or so back to our bikes, and then cycle all the way home – which was some distance – with soaking wet, freezing cold feet!). If memory serves me correctly, somewhere amid all this foolery, and as if to remind us why we had come to this godforsaken expanse in the first place, there it was …

Our river-jumping friend suddenly let out a loud cry of "Shooorrrt-eaaarrred Owwwl!" We all dutifully stopped what we were doing and aimed our binoculars in the direction of this beautiful buff-brown bird, both elegant and spectacular in equal measure. Although not a rarity as such, this was indeed a very special bird, possessing as it did something of the allure and magnetism of a stooping Peregrine or jet-fighter Merlin, while also bestowed with a silent and enigmatic grace. Some owl species are very secretive and elusive birds, and although it is not always unusual to see owls during daylight hours – especially Short-eared Owls – the association of these birds with all things 'of the night' surely adds to their awe and mystery. This creature was truly a sight to behold, roaming menacingly over this bleak and empty winter landscape. Just as soon as it had entered our world and delighted us with its presence, the owl disappeared out of sight, lost to our vision somewhere amid the wide reaches of the grassy wasteland beyond.

The Warren and Mucking

Much as we loved – or at times endured – Fobbing marshes, there were also other local spots to which we would charge off on our bikes in search of birds. Among these were what we knew as 'the Warren' and also Mucking (lovely name eh?), both near the small town of Stanford-le-Hope in Essex. Mucking's glorious claim to fame is that it has a huge landfill site which serves as a gigantic rubbish bin for the nation's capital; I don't think it has ever quite caught on as a tourist attraction though! The Warren comprised two lakes, one of them fairly large, which were managed for the benefit of anglers. A footpath ran between these two lakes, continuing across a small metal bridge that straddled a stinking muddy river, through a small reed-bed adjacent to a sewage farm, and to Mucking Church – a small, inconspicuous and rather quaint church with an overgrown graveyard. Further on was the hamlet of Mucking, and a road that snaked through the countryside to the villages of Linford and East Tilbury, and all the way to Coalhouse Fort, on the banks of the Thames beyond. Although we generally referred to the fishing lakes as the Warren, we also used both this term and Mucking interchangeably to refer to the general area comprising the lakes, the church and everything in between. The stinking muddy river, known as Mucking creek, flowed the short distance to the Thames estuary beyond, and to an area that we knew as 'the seawall'.

At the seawall there was an area of salt marsh and a very small beach. In the merciless comprehensive school humour of the day, this area therefore became known as the place where the poor kids – 'pikeys', as they were then known in our politically incorrect language – went on holiday (though I'm sure they didn't). A small road also led from the seawall back to the Warren, and adjacent to this road were a couple more fishing lakes. People also went fishing at the seawall, though it was the type of place where you were more likely to catch a submerged shopping trolley. I remember once pelting a parked car at the seawall with mud, because it belonged to a fisherman – and in our naive childhood enthusiasm, we didn't like fishermen. Not only did they impale fish on little hooks for sport, they also sometimes left discarded fishing line that was a potential death trap for our beloved birds (I once rescued a Starling at the Warren that had become hopelessly ensnared in fishing line). And lastly, some of the kids we knew from school went fishing at the Warren, and would also do such delightful things as fire stones at ducks with their catapults for 'entertainment'; some of them also collected birds' eggs, and were clearly our sworn enemies.

We would charge off on our bikes to the Warren and Mucking, with all the enthusiasm with which we ventured to the outer limits of Fobbing marshes. Upon arrival, we would ride our bikes around the larger of the two fishing lakes. This took us meandering along the network of paths used by the fisherman, and across the small rickety wooden bridges that connected the banks of the lake to a series of small islands; how we avoided taking a headfirst plunge on our bikes into the deep water on either side I'll never know. Here we saw both Reed Warblers and Sedge Warblers, though often the only clue to their presence was the incessant chattering emanating from the depths of the reeds. (As you may not be surprised to know, back then I didn't have a clue how to separate the two species by their calls alone. Thanks to an explanation by none other than Bill Oddie, on his TV series *Birding With Bill Oddie*, I have only in recent years become familiar with the subtle differences between the songs of these two birds, though even now I keep forgetting which is which.) We would also see birds such as Great Crested Grebes – not exactly exciting to most birders, though very special when you see your first one, especially in breeding plumage. I also remember seeing my first Tufted Duck, though this was on the smaller of the two lakes. I was very thrilled by these birds, as, at least to my inexperienced mind, I had seen something that was rarer and more exotic than the standard Mallards, Coots and Mute Swans. It was also a bird that we identified for ourselves: a small dark-bluish and white duck that, with an energetic leap from the surface of the water, dives with a splash and then propels itself into the depths of the lake, looking for fish (the females are not as attractive than the males, being a dull chocolate-brown colour). As its name suggests, this bird also has a conspicuous tuft gracing the back of its head. For me, therein lies one of the fundamental joys of birding: finding and identifying – for yourself – birds that you have not seen before or that are rare, elusive, impressive or special in some way. I'm not averse to seeing and enjoying birds that have been found and identified by other more knowledgeable and experienced birders, but there is surely something quite special and personally satisfying in doing it for yourself.

In addition to Reed Warblers, Sedge Warblers, Great Crested Grebes, Tufted Ducks and the usual cast of wildfowl, we also saw some other new and exciting birds at this site. We once caught a glimpse of a shy Water Rail as it briefly revealed itself on the fringe of the ever-delightful Mucking creek. No sooner had we spotted it than it crept back into the reeds – probably to die of asphyxiation. Now Water Rails are not rare, but they are extremely difficult to see, and it was not until very recently that I actually saw my second one ever. We also saw Bearded Tits in the reed-beds behind the larger of the two fishing lakes. Unlike Water Rails, these birds *are* rare, and they are usually associated with well-known RSPB reserves such as Minsmere and Titchwell. However, here at Mucking, they were dancing around in a small patch of reeds on our very own doorstep. And then there were the ever-present Skylarks, with their display flights and strangely hypnotic twittering calls, floating ever higher above the fields adjacent to the seawall, until they became mere specks amid the clouds. Sadly, Skylarks can no longer be described as 'ever-present', and like other birds of farmland and open countryside, they are now encountered far less frequently.

I also once thought I saw a Stone Curlew at the seawall. Stone Curlews are extremely rare breeding birds in the UK and can only reliably be seen in a very few areas of heath and farmland. They are summer visitors to the UK, and therefore, assuming I saw this bird in either the spring or the autumn, it is at least theoretically possible it was a Stone Curlew on migration. However, given the relatively small size of these birds, their generally nocturnal nature, and the types of habitat they characteristically frequent (i.e. heath and farmland), there is simply no way on earth that this particular bird was a Stone Curlew. With their big beady eyes, Stone Curlews are quite strange-looking, and they also appear somewhat delicate and graceful. If they had human characteristics, one could almost imagine them being rather eccentric, and not a little snobbish, perhaps wearing a monocle, and looking down their beaks at all the ever so vulgar 'ordinary birds' around them. So what self-respecting Stone Curlew would be seen dead – let alone alive – on a small dreary piece of salt marsh on the banks of the Thames, next to an oil refinery in working-class Essex, and rubbing shoulders with all those noisy, raucous gulls? The bird I saw at the seawall was clearly one of those noisy, raucous – and immature, hence the brown colour – gulls that, by a combination of youthful inexperience and rampant wishful thinking, I had embellished in my mind to the point that it had become a completely different and much rarer bird.

I did the same thing with a pipit I saw at the seawall around this time, mentally transforming it into a much rarer bird – a

Richard's Pipit if I remember correctly. In my defence though, any 'stringing' (falsely claiming a bird to be something it is not) during these early years was a result of my eager enthusiasm and strong desire to see new and exciting birds, and there was most certainly no intention on my part to simply lie about birds and pretend I had seen rarities in order to gain birding 'street-cred'. I also once thought I saw a Jack Snipe behind Mucking church, which actually could have been any small wader, or even a juvenile Snipe. This particular string was undoubtedly a result of my frantic desperation to see this particular species, as I had unfortunately missed out on a much anticipated trip to the RSPB reserve at Minsmere that my brother went on with a birding friend and his dad; I wasn't jealous though – not much! Jack Snipe was among a host of new and exciting birds that he had seen on this day and therefore now 'had over me'. The first rule of birding with your older brother is you absolutely *must not* let him see any birds that you have yet to see, especially birds that are rare, exciting, elusive or otherwise difficult to catch up with. However, should this sad set of circumstances arise, you must ensure that you make every effort to reverse this situation by seeking out these birds as soon as is humanly possibly, or he'll forever be reminding you of them, especially the rare ones, even after 20 years. He may taunt you with emails or text messages, and may even stoop so low as to get his three-year-old daughter to make you a Christmas card comprising a picture-collage of all these birds!

Of all the birds I saw at Mucking, the most exciting was the Barn Owl we encountered late one evening in flight near the church – like a silent and beautiful ghost. This was the first time I had seen the much-sought-after Barn Owl, and the feeling of exhilaration and relief at having finally seen this magnificent bird was fantastic. Although Barn Owls are not especially rare, I think even at this stage their numbers were in serious decline due to changes in agricultural practices, robbing them of their traditional nesting sites. There is also something very special about these enigmatic creatures of the night, and to see a Barn Owl in the still twilight air, and against the backdrop of an old English church… Surely this just sets the scene perfectly.

We also once found a Blue Tit's nest in the top of a hollow metal fence-post. To our delight the nest contained some fluffy little blue and yellow nestlings – all beaks and eyes and exuding cuteness. Although probably not a good idea with the benefit of hindsight, we couldn't resist picking them up and holding their warm little bodies in our hands. We did, however, put them back almost immediately, hoping that no harm would come to them.

Through our expeditions to Mucking and the surrounding areas, we also became familiar with one of the wonders of the bird world: migration. In spring we would be greeted by Swallows, House Martins and Swifts that had come all the way from Africa, and in winter by Redwings and Fieldfares just in from Scandinavia. Everyone surely has a soft spot for Swallows, Martins and Swifts, even if they cannot tell them apart. Perhaps this is because they remind us of summer, though these birds also have their own abundant charms: Swallows, with their long forked tails and flashing iridescent-blue plumage; House Martins, with their plump nestlings sticking their heads out of the familiar nests under the eaves of our houses, and then there are Swifts; those "black scimitar-winged lunatics that horde and scream above the city skyline" (Cocker, 2002) and surely make British summers just that little bit more special. On our trips to Mucking and beyond, we also became familiar with other summer migrants, such as Willow Warblers and Chiffchaffs, particularly their distinctive calls (otherwise these very similar-looking birds can be difficult to distinguish from one another).

One of the joys of birding is becoming familiar with birds that were previously unknown to you. Even if it is the most common bird in the world, the first time that you see it is very special, more so if you successfully put a name to it yourself. When I think of Mucking I don't necessarily think of the birds we saw there, nor of the fact that, in subsequent years, a Blue-Winged Teal – quite a rarity – was found there by my brother. Nor do I think of the fishing lakes, the reed-beds, the stinking river or the old churchyard. Instead, as with Fobbing marshes, I think of adventure, fun and laughs, and the pleasure of discovering and identifying new birds by ourselves; in words similar to Channel 4's inept Catholic priest *Father Ted*, "This is what it's really all about."

East Tilbury

A few miles beyond Mucking, past the villages of Linford and East Tilbury, lies Coalhouse Fort on the banks of the Thames. This is a historic fort with all the familiar gun emplacements, concrete bunkers, and impenetrable – and, believe me, unclimbable – walls and ramparts. Coalhouse Fort is a few miles downriver from Tilbury Fort, where Queen Elizabeth I made her famous "I know I have the body of a weak and feeble woman…" speech, at the time when Britain was under imminent threat of invasion at the hands of the Spanish. Adjacent to Coalhouse Fort is a long seawall that runs the length of the coast, all the way back to the Mucking area. Also adjacent to Coalhouse Fort, and immediately in front of the seawall, are a series of artificial tidal lagoons, which presumably were excavated to act as a further buffer to any flooding of the Thames (it is not far along the Thames to Canvey Island, where the infamous floods of 1953 had such a catastrophic impact). On the seaward side of these lagoons was a small band of salt marsh and tussocky grass, and then a large expanse of mudflats stretching to the Thames itself, the extent of the mudflats being entirely dependent on the level of the tide.

We knew this area simply as 'East Tilbury', and after our initial exploratory forays at Fobbing marshes and Mucking, it soon became the new focus of our birding adventures. We would head off on our bikes to Mucking for an initial perusal and then make the long journey along the country roads to East Tilbury. However, unlike Fobbing marshes and Mucking, East Tilbury was actually frequented by other local birders. These were largely middle-aged men who delighted in taking such enthusiastic adolescents as us under their wings. One of these kindly birders even lived in the same road as us, and once took my brother and me birding to another local spot, which I believe was Tilbury power station. Being a 'grown-up', he duly engaged us in proper, grown-up conversation, though I did do my best to make my brother lose his composure and erupt into laughter by constantly and surreptitiously kicking him up the backside; as 'little brother' I quite rightly considered it my duty!

Another of these birders elicited some concern among our mothers, as he was, I believe, unmarried and lived alone. At the time I couldn't make sense of these motherly concerns, though in retrospect they weren't as misplaced as I had assumed. Don't get me wrong, this birder never 'did anything' to any of us, nor ever expressed any kind of desire in this direction. However, considering our young age, some of the things he spoke to us about were – with the benefit of hindsight – somewhat inappropriate. If he was behaving in the same manner around young boys nowadays, and it came to the attention of 'the authorities', alarm bells could potentially start ringing. I should, at this point, add that, while this birder's behaviour would – in the context of today's abuse-aware (abuse-phobic?) society – likely be considered inappropriate, there is not the tiniest shred of evidence that there was any ill intent on his part. In fact, I remember him as a kindly mentor, who seemed simply to take delight in our birding enthusiasm.

Anyway, East Tilbury became very much our local patch, and by this time we had shed some – and I stress the word 'some' – of our ornithological naivety. We were respected if still inexperienced birders, and among some of the other birders at East Tilbury, we were known as the Corringham lads – hailing as we did from the small town of Corringham. Like all of our birding haunts in these formative years, East Tilbury could be quite a bleak place, especially in winter, and it took more than the regular Meadow Pipits, Cormorants, and standard gulls, wildfowl and waders to keep us happy. I remember being very pleased one winter when I spotted a group of Avocets on the mudflats. I had seen Avocets very briefly, and for the first time, on one previous occasion in Norfolk, though this was still something of a 'bogey bird' for me as a result of the birding trip to Minsmere that my brother had been on without me (Minsmere is a breeding stronghold for this bird, and is forever associated with its conservation success story). One freezing cold winter's day, we also saw a small flock of Snow Buntings in their mottled buff winter plumage. This was in the days when heavy snowfall was still a characteristic feature of winters in the south-east of England, and if memory serves me correctly, I believe there was more than a generous dusting of snow on this particular day – just to make these lovely birds feel more at home. It also made this, our very first sighting of this very scarce and rather special bird, all the more memorable.

Perhaps the best bird we saw at East Tilbury was a Great Grey Shrike, a rare if regular winter visitor to Britain, but still something to get *very* excited about. This was most definitely a first for me, though on reflection, if you ask me how I knew it wasn't a Lesser Grey Shrike – a superficially similar-looking bird – I'd have to say that I don't know. The Lesser Grey Shrike is, however, a much rarer bird, and so it is almost certain that the bird we saw was in fact a wintering Great Grey Shrike. At the time, any potential doubts about its identity were a million miles from my mind, due mainly to the fact that I had no idea that there was even such a bird as a Lesser Grey Shrike. Blissful in my ignorance, I basked in the glow of adding another bird – and a rare one at that – to my growing list of sightings. Another rarity that we saw at East Tilbury was a Glaucous Gull. I have absolutely no idea how we knew it was a Glaucous Gull, as this encounter is now a very distant – and very blurred – memory. Therefore, at the nagging and finger-prodding insistence of my conscience, I have now removed this bird from my list of sightings. Oh well, look on the bright side: this is simply one more bird to get excited about when I finally do catch up with one. I'm also reliably informed (by my brother) that we saw a Tawny Pipit – another rare bird – at East Tilbury, even going so far as to submit the sighting to the county bird recorder, who duly accepted it as genuine. Apparently this sighting was quite an event in our early birding career, though for the life of me I cannot remember a single thing about it, not even the exhilaration or smug satisfaction that I would inevitably have felt at seeing such a rare bird for the first time. Maybe I should follow the example of other birders and actually make notes of my sightings, and then perhaps I would not forget what I have seen in years to come. Then again, as well as being a very ordinary and fairly mediocre birder, I'm also quite a lazy one! It is entirely possible that what we saw was a more common pipit, and that in our enthusiasm we embellished the sighting until the bird became something it was not. However, I'm also told that other birders reported a strange-looking pipit at East Tilbury around this time, so perhaps I'm being too hard on myself, and maybe it was a Tawny Pipit after all; I will, quite simply, never know.

There was far more to do at East Tilbury than just look for birds. Coalhouse Fort was a potential goldmine of adventure and foolery for young boys, though try as I might I simply could not breach its walls. It was built to protect England from invading forces, so I have no idea why I thought I stood a chance! However, as any self-respecting young boy would, I considered it my duty to at least try, though there weren't even any trees growing in such a manner as to assist my onslaught. On the opposite side of the fort to the lagoons stood a dilapidated watchtower, which we managed to enter. This was presumably on a day when the birds were thin on the ground, or perhaps we just felt the urge to throw off all inhibitions and have some good old-fashioned fun. Atop a sturdy but crumbling base stood a large concrete observation post, with the characteristic strategically placed slits for defending soldiers both to peer and also presumably shoot through. After exploring the characteristic litter and broken-glass-strewn interior, we managed to climb up the observation post – no mean feat, as it was probably something like 8 feet in height, maybe more. At the top, a set of frighteningly rusty and fragile-looking metal steps climbed another 15 feet or so to a further concrete observation post. Of course, we couldn't resist climbing up there, though it was not a pleasant experience: I was petrified that the rusty steps would disintegrate under my feet, and that I'd either fall and injure myself horribly, or else I'd be stranded in the uppermost observation post with no way down. There is an obvious reason why adults don't do things like this: because it's bloody dangerous! But when you're a young boy with adventure on your mind, the brain tends to shut off from all rational thought. Perhaps this also explains why we also decided to while away some time hurling large stones at each other. If I remember correctly, my brother and I were in the vicinity of the lower of the two observation posts, and our birding friend was on the beach, using a large concrete block as cover from the onslaught. If, at this point, you're tempted to feel sorry for our birding friend, I should point out that this was the same 'friend' who, in the graveyard of Mucking church, fired a stone at me with a fishing catapult, hitting me square in the temple! He did, however, assure me that he didn't actually intend to hit me with the stone, and rather meant to fire past me – though I can't imagine this would have provided me with a great deal of consolation!

Wat Tyler Country Park

As its name suggests, Wat Tyler Country Park is named after the hero of the Peasants' Revolt – the ringleaders of this infamous

35

march upon the capital were, as I understand, from areas of south Essex and north Kent. The country park is situated just across the tidal creek from the outer limits of Fobbing marshes, though it was an altogether more 'user-friendly' place to spend a day's birding, boasting as it did toilets, an information centre, and even a hide overlooking a reed-fringed lake. Also, unlike Fobbing marshes, much of Wat Tyler Park comprised dense woodland and scrub thickets, criss-crossed conveniently by a series of footpaths. We saw both Cetti's Warbler and Nightingale here, or so we thought at the time; I'd now be hard-pressed to explain to anyone, including myself, how we knew for certain that they were the birds we thought they were, and both have now therefore been removed from my list of sightings – damn that troublesome conscience of mine! I did, however, see my first Long-tailed Tits at Wat Tyler – a small gang of them bobbing from branch to branch and flitting from tree to tree. These are not rare birds but they are surely just that little bit more exotic than the Blue Tits, Great Tits and even Coal Tits that many people are familiar with from their garden bird feeders. There is also the inevitable – and very welcome – tingle and feeling of satisfaction whenever you see a new bird for the first time. Delightful as these Long-tailed Tits were, the star birds at Wat Tyler were undoubtedly a group of roosting Long-eared Owls.

Acting on a tip-off, we successfully located the roost site, and were rewarded with a truly magical sight. A small group of these magnificent and elusive birds were perched in the tangled scrub, with their wings pressed hard against their elongated bodies, alert and scowling at us down their beaks for all they were worth. What a sight, and the first time any of us had seen this amazing and very exciting bird. Long-eared Owls are not rarities as such, though they are perhaps the most difficult to see of all the regular British owls. And being owls, they have all the allure and majesty of these beautiful and enigmatic creatures of the night. Yes! Long-eared Owl! Another first for the list!

We also managed to see roosting Long-eared Owls at another site in nearby Langdon Hills, though this vulnerable and isolated woodland thicket has probably long since yielded to the developers' bulldozers. Around this time, I believe I also went with my brother to see roosting Long-eared Owls at Dagenham Chase – a small oasis of scrubby open ground, surrounded by the grimy industrial and urban desert of Dagenham, on the fringes of East London. We went back there in recent years, one bitterly cold winter's day, to try our luck again, and bumped into one of the birders from our East Tilbury days. Unfortunately, we were reliably informed by this fount of local birding knowledge that the Long-eared Owls had long since departed from this site. Sadly, this birder is now deceased, though he has been afforded the high honour of having a hide at RSPB Rainham Marshes named after him.

Linford gravel pits

Birding at Linford gravel pits would sometimes be combined with trips to Mucking and East Tilbury, as the pits were located roughly halfway between the two sites, and adjacent to the Thames estuary. On one occasion we were alerted to the presence of a Little Egret at these pits. Although now quite a common sight in various parts of the UK, back in our early birding days Little Egrets were still very rare, and we raced off to savour both the rarity and the beauty of this exotic-looking bird. Despite having seen such a special bird there, Linford gravel pits will be forever etched on my mind for altogether different reasons.

Back then these were working gravel pits, with sand and gravel extraction still very much in progress. On one of our forays there, we happened upon a small conveyor belt that was up and running, and carrying small piles of sand and gravel, presumably to be processed at another part of the site. This conveyor belt stood at around waist height, and so naturally I couldn't resist jumping on it for a bit of a ride. But I had not bargained for the strength or speed of the conveyor belt's motion, and I was immediately knocked off my feet and carried along by it. This would not have been too much of a problem in itself, but I had also not bargained for the small curved metal bars that straddled the conveyor belt at regular intervals; no sooner had I regained my orientation than I became trapped by one of them. I was too big to pass underneath it, and I could not move back as the conveyor belt was continuing to carry me forward, pinning me firmly against the metal bar. As I realised I was unable to free myself, panic set in. Just as this was beginning to engulf me, our birding friend grabbed hold of me and somehow managed to wrestle me from the vice-like grip of the metal bar, and I landed rather ungraciously on the floor next to the conveyor belt. A wave of relief coursed through my veins, and I was grateful that I still had all my limbs intact and that I had been fortunate enough to have someone with me, otherwise I shudder to think what would have been my fate. My ordeal was not made any easier by the response of my brother who, rather than help to free me from my ensnarement, collapsed into hysterical laughter and continued to snigger inanely as I hobbled to my feet, vainly attempting to nurse my badly grazed back.

In the 1986 film *Withnail and I*, which has now achieved something of a cult status, Withnail's outrageously eccentric and somewhat camp Uncle Monty exclaims reminiscently:

> When I was a lad I'd rocket off on my tandem with Wrigglesworth, and we'd just ride and ride. And at night, we'd find some barn, and fall asleep with the perfumes of nature sighing on our skin (Robinson, 1989).

At the risk of over-romanticising our early birding adventures, particularly as many of the places we visited could be pretty godforsaken at times, I do think that good old Uncle Monty rather eloquently captures some of the appeal of just jumping on one's bike and exploring the natural world. Although, for adolescent boys we were pretty hardcore birders; part of the appeal of these excursions was undoubtedly the pure and unadulterated sense of adventure. I believe we discovered most of these local spots for ourselves, simply by getting on our bikes and riding off. A lot of the time we didn't even see any interesting birds, though we still kept doing it all over again. Nowadays, most young boys would probably rather stay in and play computer games all day than discover the natural world around them. And most parents would likely assume their children would be abducted and murdered if they wanted to head out to the sorts of places we frequented in those days.

Sometimes, when at the far reaches of Fobbing marshes on a freezing cold winter's day, with a mile of mud and a hundred belligerent cattle between us and the safety of our chained-up bikes, I would wonder what the hell I was doing there. And sometimes, when I feared I would be stampeded and gored to death by cattle, or that I would get cut off and drowned by a rapidly advancing tide, sink into a muddy quagmire never to be seen again, or just become hopelessly lost, I yearned for the warm safety of my home. But, looking back on these experiences, I think I was lucky to have had such an opportunity to explore the natural world and its delights, an opportunity which I fear is sadly precluded by the lifestyles of many of today's youth.

Further afield

Canvey Point

One of my earliest memories of birding further afield was when we persuaded our biology teacher to take a group of us on a weekend birding trip to Canvey Island. Admittedly this only just qualifies as 'further afield', being as it is only several miles downriver from East Tilbury. Canvey Island is not the most glamorous of places; it comprises housing estates for the largely working class population, industrial estates, a poor excuse for a high street, plus a caravan park, a nightclub, and a few awful amusement arcades – in reality, a bit of a poor man's Southend-on-Sea. It does, however, boast miles of seawall and a fairly large stretch of tidal salt marsh, and it was to this area rather than its other abundant delights that we eagerly headed.

My only real memories of this trip are my terror at the prospect of being stranded by the advancing tide, a real possibility if you lingered for too long, and also of another new and exciting bird that we saw. The aforementioned 'inappropriate' birder of East Tilbury fame also accompanied us on this trip, and amid the usual cast of waders and gulls, he suddenly cried out, "That's a skua, that's an Arctic Skua!" We all turned our heads to see this dull-brown pirate of the seas swooping across the seashore like a raptor. Of the four regular British species of skua, the Arctic Skua is usually the most often encountered, though to see even this bird you have to be in the right place and with the weather conditions very much on your side. Skuas are also imbued with a dark and menacing glamour which makes them rather exciting, especially when they twist and turn in aerial pursuit of an unfortunate tern – which will, quite rightly, be somewhat reluctant to part with its hard-earned catch of fish. Although the skua was located and identified by another birder, the satisfaction of adding a new and exciting bird to my growing repertoire of sightings almost made the ever-present fear of getting drowned by the encroaching tide a price worth paying.

Hanningfield and Abberton Reservoirs

Hanningfield reservoir in mid-Essex was, unfortunately, out of bounds to members of the public without a permit – the part of it that we went to was anyway. Such things didn't usually worry us though, and we overcame this simply by climbing over the fence, while keeping a wary eye out for any angry water bailiffs heading our way. Although my memories of birding at Hanningfield have now faded almost to the point of non-existence, I am reliably informed that our breaking and entering was rewarded with sightings of Ruddy Duck. This attractive duck – the males with their reddish-brown bodies and shiny blue bills – is an American species that was introduced to the UK in the 1940s. While not rare, their populations in the UK are nevertheless localised, and, at such an early stage in our birding career, this would have been a very special and also very exciting encounter, not to mention my first ever sighting of this species.

We also once found a Herring Gull at Hanningfield that was decidedly under the weather. We captured the gull and, despite its best attempts to bite our fingers off, took it to a middle-aged acquaintance of ours, who unofficially operated his own bird hospital. The diagnosis was botulism, a kind of food poisoning, though the story had a happy ending with the gull being successfully nursed back to health.

Abberton reservoir was somewhat further afield, in north Essex, and my only sojourn here was in order to see a bird that combined both rarity and glamour in equal measure: a Red-footed Falcon. Much to my joy, it was still present upon our arrival, and we enjoyed fantastic views of this splendid bird perched on a fence-post for all to see. This is the only Red-footed Falcon I have ever seen, and on a recent visit to the RSPB

41

reserve at Minsmere, in an attempt to see another, we 'dipped' – failing to see it. We did, however, manage to see a rather beautiful Grass Snake, which did its best to make up for the absence of the falcon. One of the many good things about Minsmere is that you can at least console yourself with a visit to the café, followed by a stroll around the shop – ah yes, the joys of being nearly middle-aged!

Elmley

The first proper birding place I went to was Elmley RSPB reserve, on the Isle of Sheppey in north Kent. As I had missed out on the trip to Minsmere that my brother had been taken on, I naturally jumped at the chance of visiting Elmley. I was keen to make up for lost time, not to mention missed birds, and I was therefore somewhat miffed when I failed to notice some Marsh Harriers that another birder had seen on the long walk to the reserve itself. My brother had seen Marsh Harriers at Minsmere, so I *had* to see this bird as soon as possible!

Elmley can be quite a bleak place, and the long walk out on the track, which meanders for a mile or so across the rough grazing land to the reserve, can be pretty tiring. It can also be quite draining of one's birding motivation. In recent years, I have been known to walk out to the reserve and, after a quick scan for Peregrines and Merlins, think "sod this" and then walk all the way back to the car; the additional few hundred yards or so to the first hide was just that little bit too much without the prospect of something exciting, and I have never actually made it to the farthest hide, which is quite a hike.

Anyway, back then there was no stopping my youthful enthusiasm. On one particular occasion, our long walk out to the hides was rewarded with the spectacle of a stunning Spoonbill, and another time with a lovely Red-necked Phalarope swimming daintily on the surface of the shallow lagoons. Both species are quite rare if regular birds, and both were undoubtedly firsts for my list. We would also very likely have seen wintering Hen Harriers and Short-eared Owls at Elmley. The same is also true of the Little Owl that, I'm reliably informed, we saw behind the reserve toilets. I have seen both Hen Harriers and Short-eared Owls since this time, though Little Owls, I'm afraid, continue to elude me. My brother also assures me that I was with him when he saw a Little Owl years ago in his friend's garden amid the local arable farmland, though I cannot remember this at all. Oh well, at least when I do finally catch up with a Little Owl, the sighting will be all the more special.

We also saw quite a well-known birder at Elmley: John Gooders. To us he was primarily known for having been co-contestant with Bill Oddie in the 'Big Bird Race' of 1983 – a race between two teams of birders to tick off the most species of birds in the UK in a single day. We did not, alas, have the bottle to talk to the great man, though this chance sighting did whet our appetites for a subsequent meeting with two birding legends in Norfolk: Bill Oddie and Bryan Bland. Bill Oddie was – to us in those days – a birding icon, and we had all but elevated his *Little Black Bird Book* to the status of birding scripture. The long-bearded Bryan Bland was quite a well-known birder, and in his birding uniform of smock, shorts and sandals, was seemingly immune to the very worst that the British weather could sling at him. Maybe he's like one of those tough old fell-runners I've encountered in subsequent years who, as I'm wheezing and spluttering my way agonisingly slowly up a steep windswept mountain in the freezing cold and pouring rain, proceed to run past at full pelt in only shorts and a t-shirt, and then disappear into the mist, having hardly even broken sweat. I'm sure they only do it to humiliate us mere mortals.

North Norfolk

The title page of our copy of *Bill Oddie's Gone Birding* bears some squiggly writing that reads 'Cheers to Pete and Andrew, Bill Oddie', underneath which my brother has written neatly

'Bill Oddie (Cley 31ˢᵗ May 86)'. The man himself signed our book! And as if that wasn't enough, if you turn the page, underneath the formal blurb announcing the name of the publisher and year of copyright etc., further – though less squiggly – writing reads 'Happy birding, Bryan Bland', with 'Bryan Bland – Cley 86' again appended by my brother. Bryan Bland as well as Bill Oddie! We had bumped into these two birding heroes of ours at a bird fair at Cley – that most legendary of Norfolk birding spots – by pure chance. I'm not sure how we knew of Bryan Bland at the time, but he is still quite a well-known birder today and is easily identifiable by his long beard of Old Testament proportions, and his characteristic scanty get-up, even in weather that would make a Himalayan Yeti stay indoors. He must have been quite taken aback when confronted by two eager young birding autograph-hunters, and, obliging though he was, he clearly didn't feel that his birding status warranted such attention. His exact reply when asked for his squiggle was, "Yes, but why?" My brother happened upon him again in recent years, though was horrified to see that he was wearing – wait for it – long trousers and boots! This, naturally, shattered my brother's illusions of the great man, prompting him to send a text message that read something like 'Bryan Bland in long trousers and boots shocker!' I can't remember much else about this particular day in Norfolk, except that we proudly had our photo taken with both Oddie and Bland. I also remember that, as with most of our birding trips at this time, we were chauffeur-driven by our parents – good old parents.

On another occasion our dad took us on a day trip to Cley to see what I believe was only the UK's second ever Little Whimbrel. After a long and fretful car journey, we did at last manage to feast our eyes on the star attraction. However, apart from the fact that this was the rarest bird I had ever seen, I don't recall much about the sighting itself. I do, however, remember spending the preceding week in a state of nervous agitation, willing the weekend to approach and agonising over whether the bird would still be there. Such visible agitation in anticipation of seeing a rare bird, or – more to the point – the unthinkable prospect of *not* seeing it, is an oft-quoted theory as to the derivation of the word 'twitcher', and I am filled with pride to think that I went on a bona fide twitch at such a young and tender age. This was long before the days of rare bird phone lines, pager services and Internet communication, and at a time when the birding grapevine still operated by word of mouth. The centre of this birding grapevine – not just for Norfolk, but for pretty much the entire country it seems – was Nancy's café in the village of Cley-next-the-Sea, on the north Norfolk coast. Mark Cocker, in *Birders: Tales of a Tribe* (2001), describes Nancy's as 'legendary', and goes on to state that:

> Every birder knew of it. Most birders of sufficient age visited it. Many went there weekly. Some almost lived there. One or two actually did. And even those who never went there spoke to its occupants on a regular basis… When the café finally closed, the event was recorded in the press and on regional and national TV. I believe it should now have one of those blue English Heritage plaques commemorating its former status.

While I cannot claim to have had anything to do with the place, we did go there on one occasion to pay homage to such a birding institution. It must have been when there were no birds around, or else when everyone was out birding rather than sitting around talking about birds, as all I remember is sitting in the garden at the back with the hordes of other birders conspicuously notable by their absence.

As well as seeing my first Avocets in Norfolk – another bird that my brother 'had over me' from that fateful trip to Minsmere without me – and visiting the Walsey Hills bird observatory, another memory I have from around this time is going on a trip to Norfolk for the day with our local RSPB group. Despite the horrendous nausea-inducing coach journey, we had a great time at the then Norfolk Naturalists Trust (now Norfolk Wildlife Trust) reserve at Holme-next-the-Sea. I remember strolling wistfully along the wide and beautiful expanse of beach and seeing some excellent birds. We saw a Great Skua and Manx Shearwater out to sea, a Red-breasted Flycatcher (or 'R B Flicker' as it was rather irritatingly abbreviated) in the pines near the bird observatory, a Wryneck and a male Red-backed Shrike, perched characteristically on a barbed wire fence, and no doubt looking for some unfortunate creature to impale. What a day: new birds aplenty, and at least three of them – the Flycatcher, Shrike and Wryneck – genuine rarities. On the coach journey home, I entertained myself by throwing bits of food at the birder on the seat behind me who was asleep, and my brother entertained himself – though nobody else – by continuously letting off the most evil-smelling odours, which likely made me feel even sicker than I already did. Although I was able to use it against him the next time he was in trouble with our parents, and he was given the sternest of lectures about his immature behaviour.

Dungeness

Dungeness, or 'Dunge' as we knew it, is a unique place. It comprises mile upon mile of shingle, which forms an enormous spit jutting way out into the English Channel. Amid this vast landscape are endless tangled gorse bushes, a couple of lighthouses, and a small line of eccentric and storm-battered little shacks – the type of place you'd expect to find some mad old seadog, like Uncle Albert in *Only Fools and Horses*, making his living by selling maritime memorabilia or antique anchors, or else a family of dreadlocked hippies trying to get away from it all. And all this is set against the backdrop of the vast nuclear power station. I always find Dungeness to be a very strange and sometimes unsettling combination of beauty and bleakness, and there is most definitely an almost lunar feel to it. Even Bill

Oddie (1983) describes it, perhaps with somewhat less restraint, as a "… wasteland, a strange desolate landscape that looked like a vision of earth after a nuclear holocaust."

There are three primary locations of interest to birders at Dungeness. Firstly, there is the RSPB reserve, which comprises a series of shallow lakes of the type favoured by waders and wildfowl, surrounded by the omnipresent shingle and gorse. Secondly, there is the bird observatory nestled immediately behind the power station and in an area of intermittent gorse and scrub, not far from the headland of the vast shingle spit. And then there is the enormous bank of pebbles overlooking the steeply inclined beach, both of which are squeezed between the looming concrete of the power station and the vastness of the sea beyond. Unlike Bill Oddie, I have never stayed at the observatory, nor have I even visited it. I have, nevertheless, sampled Dungeness's other delights.

My only memory of the RSPB reserve from this time is seeing my first Smew, a type of duck, including the dashingly beautiful black-and-white male. A trip to Dungeness is not complete, however, without a spot of seawatching from atop the vast bank of pebbles in front of the nuclear power station. As well as the bitterly cold weather, I remember seeing my first Common Scoter, and also a possible Great Northern Diver out to sea here, the latter in particular being a fairly scarce bird, and not at all easy to see. There were also the usual manic flocks of gulls and terns, gorging themselves on the fish attracted close inshore by the warm cooling water pumped out from the power station – in birding parlance this area being known as 'the patch'. I also remember Dunge because it was on the way there that we once stopped at Bedgebury Pinetum, a lovely area of woodland in Kent. Here I saw my first and only Hawfinch, a very beautiful and elusive bird. As with many of my sightings in these early years, had I known then how difficult it would subsequently prove to catch up with such birds again, I would surely have appreciated the experience all the more.

Thursley Common

Despite its rather understated title of Common, this 800-acre NNR in Surrey is a beautiful expanse of open heath, bog and woodland, with dense tracts of twisted gorse bushes and lizards basking in the sun on the reserve's boardwalks. We were here specifically to see Hobbies, and see them we did. We were mesmerised as these handsome slate-grey falcons with their characteristic red trousers dashed across the open heath above our heads in aerial pursuit of dragonflies and other unfortunate winged creatures. Yes! Another new bird, and such a spectacular and exciting one. Hobbies were also much less frequently encountered in the early 80s than they are now, which made the sighting all the more special.

Another highlight of the day was an encounter with a Dartford Warbler, a rare breeding species confined to a limited number of sites in the south of England. The bird we saw was clearly in a co-operative mood, sitting proudly atop a gorse bush in characteristic pose, as if wantonly expecting a field-guide illustrator to come by at any moment, with brush and easel at the ready. We duly savoured the moment, though in retrospect not nearly enough, as my recent attempts to track down this species on the vast tracts of open heathland in the New Forest had ended in abject failure.

As with quite a few of our birding outings back then, our trip to Thursley Common was courtesy of our long-suffering parents. There was, however, a downside to parental involvement on this occasion, as our mum cast a sizeable dark cloud over the otherwise radiant sunshine of the open heath with one of the most foul and prolonged moods we have ever been subjected to; at least she didn't scare the birds off though.

Minsmere

The famous RSPB reserve at Minsmere was, and still is, a magnet for enthusiastic young birders. In my early birding days, it offered the chance of catching up with the extremely rare Marsh Harrier, plus a whole host of other birding treats. Given the trauma of having missed out on the previous trip to Minsmere (the one my brother had been on), it had been assigned an almost mythic status in my fevered and rampantly jealous imagination. It was a place of which I had heard tantalising and exotic tales, though with each passing day, week, month and maybe even year, I also feared I would never feast my earthly eyes upon this Camelot of the birding world. Logic therefore informs me that, while in the hides on my first trip there, I would have been salivating and rubbing my hands with glee over every bird I saw that my brother had already seen from his previous trip, each of these sightings indelibly seared on my consciousness for all eternity. Certainly I must have seen Marsh Harrier for the first time, thereby going some way to wiping the smug grin from my brother's face. But, odd as it seems, I don't remember a single thing about this visit. Maybe this is because, in my heart of hearts, I knew that the Jack Snipe I once thought I saw at Mucking was not a Jack Snipe after all, and that my brother therefore still had this bird over me from that fateful trip to Minsmere without me. Perhaps, having failed to see this bird on my own first trip there, I was struck with the realisation that the image of my brother's smirking face would always haunt me. Maybe the thought of this was so traumatic that my mind has now permanently erased all memory of my first day's birding at Minsmere. Or perhaps it is simply because – again – I was too lazy to take notes of my sightings.

We went on other birding excursions in these formative years, either courtesy of our parents, the parents of birding friends, or by coach with the local RSPB group. We went to the Naze on the north Essex coast, where we saw numbers of dainty Sanderlings scurrying to keep one step ahead of the ever-encroaching tide, plus my first ever Puffin, bobbing on the cold winter sea. We went to the brecks of East Anglia to see Stone

Curlews, a rare breeding bird confined to only a handful of UK sites. We also went to Rutland Water in Leicestershire, though unfortunately didn't see anything much to write home about, and this was long before the Osprey reintroduction project of recent years. And an Osprey would have done just nicely, especially as it would take me another 25 years or so to finally catch up with one.

Even further afield

Somerset and Exmoor

My family always stayed in the UK for our annual holiday, and going to such far-flung places as the West Country and the Lake District clearly provided us with a golden opportunity to add to our ever-growing list of birds.

On our way to Butlin's at Minehead in Somerset, I remember being overjoyed at seeing my very first Pheasant, a bird that my brother saw during his trip to Minsmere without me. We would also have seen our first Buzzards – if not from the car on the long journey west, then wheeling majestically over the wilds of Exmoor. And as if that wasn't enough, we also saw a spectacular Merlin dashing across the roadside moors as we were driving along in the car. Virtually all memory of this has now faded, and the passage of time, combined with my rampaging conscience, has significantly eroded the integrity of this sighting in my mind.

If, at this point, it seems that I'm being too hard on myself, a colossal string was only just around the corner. This was in the form of a Montagu's Harrier – a very rare bird – I convinced myself we'd seen from the window of our chalet in Minehead. It certainly looked like a harrier. My bird books mentioned that one of the clues indicating a Montagu's Harrier sighting was the time of year it is seen, i.e. summer, which it was. Looking back, I have no idea what this bird was, though the chances of it being a Montagu's are pretty much nil. Maybe it was a Hen Harrier. Maybe it was a Curlew, whose enormous down-curved bill was not visible through my bins at such a distance. Maybe it was just a huge immature gull doing a good impression of a harrier. Or maybe it was even a pigeon on its way to a fancy dress party, decked out in a Montagu's outfit! One thing's for sure though, it was most definitely *not* a Montagu's Harrier!

The Lake District

Another to me notorious string from around this time was the Goshawk we thought we saw in steep aerial descent over the rolling green landscape of the Lake District. We reasoned that, because this bird was buzzard-sized, though to our inexperienced eyes was not behaving like a Buzzard, it must have been a Goshawk. Goshawks are not only quite scarce, they are also extremely secretive and notoriously difficult to see. Although it is within the realms of possibility that this bird was indeed a Goshawk, it is extremely unlikely; it was probably a Buzzard which thought it would have a bit of a laugh at the expense of a couple of over-eager young whippersnappers.

On this holiday we saw our first ever Dipper – a bird that is always a delight to behold – together with the usual supporting cast of excitable Grey Wagtails. Buzzards wheeled over the fells with their characteristic upheld wings and cat-like mewing calls, and we also saw our first and only Pied Flycatcher flitting around in the roadside trees. Best of all though, and a fitting reward after a long uphill slog, was a pair of Peregrines patrolling the undulating hillside atop a steep and densely vegetated cliff face. We were further rewarded on our descent with cracking views of one of these magnificent birds perched on the cliff; they may well have had a clutch of eggs, or even a couple of hungry chicks stashed away in a crevice high in the rock face. Another memorable sighting from this holiday was the spectacle of our mum performing a classic banana-skin style slip on a piece of wet ground in the Langdale Valley, subsequently landing rather unceremoniously on her backside. My brother and I laughed hysterically and deservedly incurred the fearsome wrath of our angry parents.

On this holiday we also visited the seabird colony at St. Bee's Head on the Cumbria coast. As well as the usual Guillemots, Razorbills, Kittiwakes and Fulmars, these sandstone cliffs were also known as a breeding site for the rare Black

Guillemot. Unfortunately, we had not done our homework nearly well enough, and had visited this site too late in the season after all the seabirds had left. I don't know whether we would have seen any birds anyway, even if we had come earlier in the year, as our mum had a panic attack every time we ventured within a 100 yards of the cliff edge; unlike us, she clearly didn't think certain death was a risk worth taking if it meant we saw Black Guillemots.

The Isles of Scilly

Among our various family holidays during these years, the jewel in the crown was undoubtedly a mouth-watering and much anticipated trip to the Isles of Scilly (also known as the Scilly Isles, the Scillies or even just Scilly), off the south-west coast of Cornwall. The Scillies were, and still are – together with Fair Isle at the opposite end of the UK – *the* place to see exotic and heart-stoppingly rare wind-blown vagrants, and to which all serious birders are, at some point in their lives, almost duty-bound to make a pilgrimage. I have no idea how we persuaded our ever-obliging parents to take us by taxi into central London, by train all the way from London to Penzance, and then on a long and nauseous boat ride out into the Atlantic Ocean. But persuade them we did, and so, one memorable day in October 1986, we set sail for that veritable Mecca of UK birding.

We stayed in a Bed and Breakfast in Hugh Town on St. Mary's, the largest of the inhabited islands. It was from here that news of the latest rarities would be dispersed to the Scillies' transient population of roving birders. My brother and I were as excited as a bunch of students at a party with a free bar, and lost no time at all in frantically chasing after any rarities we heard news of. A Semi-palmated Sandpiper, otherwise known as 'semi-pee', was picked up quite easily, and we also managed to see Yellow-browed Warbler, Little Bunting, Firecrest and Richard's Pipit. We caught a boat to the neighbouring island of Tresco for the Rose-breasted Grosbeak, which we thankfully managed to observe amongst a huddle of other birders. We also returned to this island later in the holiday when news broke of a Grey-cheeked Thrush, an extremely rare American vagrant.

It was touch and go whether we would ever get a chance to see this bird, as our parents initially refused to let us take the boat on our own due to the rough seas. Fortunately, they eventually acquiesced to our pleadings, on the condition that they came with us. To this day our mum still speaks of that boat crossing as if she'd braved a near shipwreck amid 100-foot waves in the storm-lashed Antarctic seas. We eventually saw the Grey-cheeked Thrush, though only after performing a timely sprint, followed by some last-minute commando-style dives, tumbles and rolls, which, to our immense relief, secured a great view of the bird in a garden prior to it disappearing from view.

This poor bird had been blown all the way across the Atlantic Ocean – probably almost dying of exhaustion in the process – only to find itself lost and all alone in a strange and faraway land. And just when it needed to rest and recuperate after its traumatic ordeal, it found itself mercilessly pursued and harassed by the khaki-clad, binocular-wearing, tripod-wielding visitors to of this distant place. And, to add insult to injury, just when this wretched creature thought its luck simply had to take a turn for the better…it found itself in the jaws of one of the local cats! It was here that it sadly took its final breath, no doubt sighing to itself 'goodbye cruel world'. Such was the interest in this bird and its unfortunate demise that it even made it into the national newspapers.

There was an even bigger and more frantic onslaught of birders when news broke of an Upland Sandpiper on the golf course on St. Mary's. The course was duly invaded by hordes of birders, though, much to our relief, we did at least manage to see the bird before it either flew away or was trampled to death under myriad pairs of wellies. At the time, I enjoyed such rough-and-tumble, high-speed birding pursuits, and I got a buzz from rubbing shoulders with the 'top boys' at the cutting edge of birding. I also believed wholeheartedly that twitchers did not deserve to be demonised in the way that they sometimes were, i.e. as irresponsible, tick-hungry lunatics who would wantonly damage property, the countryside and sometimes even the health of the birds themselves in pursuit of their quarry. Nowadays, though, I'm not so sure.

I nearly went to the Scillies again last year (2006) with my then girlfriend (now wife), but opted instead to spend a week birding in north Norfolk. As well as financial considerations, part of our decision to go to Norfolk rather than the Scillies was that we didn't fancy spending the entire holiday chasing after rarities. This can be pretty stressful at times, especially when you dip, meaning that the preceding state of tension and nervous anticipation is not even rewarded in any way. Such rarity-chasing would also have rendered us almost totally dependent upon the identification skills of other birders rather than our own. If I'm not familiar enough with a bird to identify it straight away, and it's not featured in any of my trusted field guides, then I'm as lost as the afore-mentioned Grey-cheeked Thrush.

Anyway, our holiday on the Scillies was rounded off in true style with the news that we would be unable to board either the *Scillonian*, the passenger ferry to Penzance, or the helicopter due to a severe bout of stormy weather. Together with another family, we therefore chartered a small plane. Once airborne, we were afforded spectacular views of the storm-lashed islands, deep blue sea and, after some half-an-hour or so, compared to something like two hours aboard the *Scillonian*, the rocky headland of Land's End. Despite a rather terrifying landing during which I was convinced the plane would plunge off the cliffs and into the sea, this was what I called travelling in style.

The wilderness years

I don't quite know how or why it happened, but after a few years spent chasing after every bird we could set eyes on, my brother's and my obsession with birding started to fade, and after a while fizzled out altogether. There was no particular reason for this, and it happened over a period of time. I think the best explanation is that, as we were plunged headlong into our early and then mid-teens, birding simply gave way to other priorities and interests in our lives, and the fun of rushing off on our bikes with our mates, especially on a cold or rainy day, ceased to hold out the promise of adventure and pleasure it once did. Our early birding adventures did, nevertheless, foster a keen interest in and deep appreciation of wildlife and the natural world, which would keep me sustained over the next 18 years or so, until I finally got back into birding.

If you go down to the woods today...

Despite its proximity to the sprawling housing estates of Basildon, that veritable hub of all things quintessentially 'Essex', Langdon Hills Country Park is surprisingly lovely. It comprises fairly large tracts of mixed woodland and open fields, interspersed with a series of footpaths and bridleways. One of my earliest memories of Langdon Hills, from my early birding years, was finding this dazzling, jewel-like blue wing feather from a Jay, a bird whose familiarity belies its beauty. As well as being mesmerised by the brilliance of this feather, I also felt a sense of achievement that I was able to put a name to the bird that it belonged to. I held onto the feather for dear life, and stashed it away at home like a shiny piece of treasure. In time, this duly took pride of place in our burgeoning feather collection – a somewhat more savoury pursuit than collecting birds' wings.

In my post-birding teenage years, I well remember having a deep reverence for nature that, in retrospect, simply oozed notions of youthful idealism. There was a time when I would go to Langdon Hills every weekend, sometimes on my bike. At other times I would be dropped off and then picked up later by my parents. Once among the trees, I would not only explore the forest to my heart's content, but also fantasise about what it would have been like before humans colonised Britain, when the ancient woodlands literally spread the length and breadth of the British Isles, and almost to the top of every mountain – paradise! I also fantasised about what it would be like to live in such a forested wilderness, in a so-called primitive culture such as the Amazonian Indians, who live in relative harmony with the natural world around them and, like me, have a deep reverence for, and love of, nature. However, while on my lone woodland adventures, my head wasn't always in the clouds, and I would still keep an eye out for any interesting birds or animals.

On some of my woodland visits I would leave the path altogether and simply head off into the trees. I would walk, clamber and sometimes even crawl through the vegetation until, eventually, I came out to some path or other familiar landmark. It was on one such early foray at One Tree Hill, part of Langdon Hills Country Park, that I saw my first Tawny Owl, a bird that had so far managed to elude me. I was walking through the woods, away from any footpath or bridleway, when I noticed with great surprise a plump and rather feline-looking bird roosting in the tree above me. I felt very privileged to see such a beautiful bird at close quarters, and one that, rather like the Badger or the Fox, is such a well-known symbol of our native wildlife. Despite its abundance in the UK, Tawny Owls are not at all easy to see, unless you know of a specific nest or roost site, and I relished the sight of this lovely little fellow tucked up against the tree, asleep. I would have appreciated this sighting all the more had I known that it would be at least another 20 years before I saw another, and that this would be only a very fleeting glimpse of an indistinct brown object flying away from me into a dense tangle of trees. I even failed to catch up with Tawny Owls on a recent visit to a very well-known roost site in Norfolk, and I am now of the view that these birds most definitely have it in for me.

On another such lone woodland foray, I was once again walking quite a way off the beaten track. Suddenly, as if from nowhere, a large brown bird exploded into the air almost from beneath my feet, and flew for all it was worth, deeper into the woods. Despite the fact that this flurry of wings and feathers had scared me almost to death, I knew instantly what this bird was: a Woodcock. These are very elusive birds and not at all easy to see, and unless you accidentally flush one out, as I had, they are best seen in their breeding areas at dusk, when male birds engage in their characteristic patrol flights, known as 'roding'. I had seen a Woodcock previously during the height of my birding years, though this was a chance sighting of one flying over – of all places – our back garden! This was in the depths of winter, so the bird was probably forced out of its usual environment by a desperate need for food. Despite the fact that I no longer actively went out birding, I still knew a damn good bird when I saw one.

Another memorable woodland sighting, again at Langdon Hills, was with my brother – at about 4am in the morning. I had just returned home, having done some night work, erecting seating equipment at a local sports centre that also doubled as a conference venue. I was meant to be a full-time student at a local further education college. But as I had already completed my 6th-form studies and secured a place at university, I preferred to bunk off from college and earn some money so that I could save up for my proper student years ahead. My brother was awake when I arrived home in the early hours. We decided to head off to Langdon Hills to watch the sun come up and hopefully catch sight of some exciting woodland creature or other, more especially badgers. We quickly got our things together and drove off in my rather clapped-out antique chocolate-brown Chrysler Avenger, affectionately known by one of my mates as the 'Brown-mobile'. In the gloomy pre-dawn light, we trekked through the woods to a spot that maybe – just maybe – would give us a grandstand view of something very special indeed.

Shortly after we arrived and made ourselves comfortable, we were rewarded with what we had come to see. A family of Badgers, including a small gang of cubs, made their way out from a sett among the roots of the trees and started to sniff around. They seemed totally oblivious to our presence, and the cubs duly began to play and mess around with each other; they were fairly large cubs, perhaps the equivalent of primary-school-age, and so this must have been their early morning playtime. It was indeed a magical sight, one that I had never before seen, nor have since. Once we had had our fill of the Badgers' antics we headed off to nearby One Tree Hill, where we sat overlooking the Thames Estuary below us in the gathering daylight and enjoyed the rabbits scurrying around in the early morning stillness.

Taking to the hills

At my brother's urging, who had been on the same trip two years previously and couldn't recommend the experience enough, I went on a week's hillwalking trip to the Isle of Skye in Scotland. This was organised by the 6th-form college I attended at the time where I completed a course in Environmental studies and Geology. I had previously walked among the hills and crags of the Lake District on our family holiday and also in the Yorkshire Dales as part of my A-Level Geography field trip. This would, however, be my first opportunity to actually climb a genuine mountain. I couldn't wait. Simply glimpsing the spectacular Scottish hills from the window of the minibus was exhilarating, especially as we wound our way through the majestic and rocky grandeur of Kintail in the West Highlands.

When we finally got among the imposing black Gabbro rock of the mighty Cullin ridge on the Isle of Skye, I felt like I had entered another world.

This was a world of enormous rock buttresses rising eerily out of the thick mist, like the mighty ramparts of a dreaded and impenetrable castle; a land of steep rock faces and precarious narrow ridges, where one slip on the shiny wet rocks could send you falling into the depths of the cold white mist below; a harsh world of bitter winds and driving rain, whose enormity of scale brought into stark contrast the frailty of human society compared to the might of the natural world; a world where the very building blocks of our so-called civilised world – laws, money, taxes, transport infrastructure, offices, paperwork – seemed utterly meaningless. Quite simply, this was a world where I felt alive – alive in a way that I had never felt before.

The landscape of Skye took my breath away, and I instantly fell in love with its brooding mountains and steep rocky coasts. And as I was still taking it all in while walking through a tract of pine forest perched on the edge of the coast, along came a bird so spectacular and awe-inspiring that it could not have chosen a more inspiring backdrop. It was circling high over the water, its enormous flat wings giving it the appearance of a huge flying door. As if in homage to my growing approbation, this magnificent creature came closer in towards us, flying ever lower until it eventually landed in one of the pine trees behind us. And there it sat for all to see, with its enormous feathered bulk, ferocious-looking bill and creamy brown head feathers. It was none other than a White-tailed Eagle. The considerable annoyance of not having brought any binoculars with me was only slightly offset by the fact that one of the leaders had a monocular (single eyepiece) with him, and my bulging eye strained through this for all it was worth. Even though I was no longer the enthusiastic young birder I once was, I still knew what a truly amazing sight this was. White-tailed Eagles are not only rare, having become extinct in the UK prior to their reintroduction programme of recent years, they are also of an enormity that simply leaves one in a state of wide-eyed awe. And as if all that wasn't enough, I could hardly have asked for a better backdrop of mountain, sea and wide-open skies against which to view such a wondrous beast. This more than made up for the trip to Minsmere I had missed out on in my early birding years. And to make it just that little bit more special, to this day my brother has still not seen a White-tailed Eagle. Ah, sweet revenge!

Our week on Skye, during which we ascended two of the peaks on the monstrous Cullin ridge, was rounded off perfectly with a night spent under the stars. We spent all day walking to a remote coastal inlet at the foot of the ridge. Once there, we cooked food on our stoves and then spent the night in bivvy bags. It was one of the most moving experiences of my entire life. As well as the dark grandeur of the mighty Cullins, the very act of casting off all the shackles of the civilised world and returning, even for one night, to a very basic way of living made me feel somehow that I had returned home, to where I belonged. Although this place was frequented by hillwalkers, and even boasted a stone hut (whose steel shutters you could presumably unlock if you belonged to the right organisation), the remoteness was such that it felt as if we were the first humans ever to have set foot there. A group of curious seals even followed me as I made my way around the inlet to find fresh water, as if they were trying in some way to interact with me. Later that night I lay in my bivvy bag, my head poking out into the cold night air. Beyond the faint silhouette of the ridge high above, the skies were filled with thousands of stars, all twinkling bright against the deep inky blackness beyond. And as I lay there utterly mesmerised, as if to remind me that the show wasn't quite over, a shooting star streaked across the night sky, leaving a sparkling trail of silver in its wake. This place was quite simply spellbinding.

After this life-changing trip to the Isle of Skye, hillwalking became my new passion in which I indulged with a vengeance whenever possible. I went to Snowdonia as part of a Sport and Leisure Studies course I was doing at college, and also to the Lake District with one of my mates. I also went to the Isle of Arran in Scotland on an A-Level Geology field trip. Alas, I could only stare wistfully at the mountains from afar, though, as we picked our way through Arran's coastal rock formations, the flocks of Eider did their best to cheer me up with their soothing and also rather comical cooing calls, calls which have also been likened to the rather effeminate utterances of Frankie Howerd. As well as being rather fitting symbols of the rugged and beautiful Scottish coast all about us, Eiders are very attractive birds, especially the males in their plush black, white and lime-green finery.

At the end of my 6th-form studies, I booked myself onto a mountaineering course based in Scotland. I had successfully persuaded my college to partly fund this by pleading my case as an aspirant outdoor pursuits instructor. The north face of Ben Nevis was on an almost Alpine scale and every bit as inspiring as the dark and mighty buttresses, ridges and pinnacles of the Cullins on Skye. Although the worsening weather meant a planned ascent of Tower Ridge had to be aborted, we did – after much gasping for breath and near mental and physical collapse on my part – make it to the rock-strewn summit of 'the mighty Ben'. On our snaking descent, which didn't quite deliver the relief that I had so longed for, I was cheered by the spectacle of a small group of Ptarmigan in their beautiful mottled autumnal plumage, so ingeniously camouflaged amid the rocks and snow. I saw similarly clad Ptarmigan on the high slopes of Buchaille Etive Mor in Glencoe, and it was from here that I also observed what I thought was a Golden Eagle, soaring over the mighty Aonach Eagach ridge looming beyond. In retrospect, I think our learned instructor may have been correct in his assessment of differentiating between Golden Eagles and Buzzards: if it's too far away to tell whether it's a Buzzard or a Golden Eagle, then it's an eagle. Although it is entirely possible that this bird was a Golden Eagle, in all likelihood it was probably just a Buzzard, trying its best to convince me that it was something bigger and better.

The wonder of Wales: university years

In September 1991, my parents drove my brother and me all the way to Aberystwyth in mid-Wales, on the coast of Cardigan Bay. In a week's time I was due to start university to read for a degree in Earth Studies. I was almost unbearably excited – not at the prospect of studying and writing essays, but of this big adventure that lay ahead. I was excited at the prospect of finally leaving home and being independent, of making new friends and not having to kick around on my own as I had done for the last year. And most of all, I was excited at the prospect of finally leaving behind the gloomy world of singledom, and hopefully meeting the girl of my dreams. (Don't ask me why, but I'm suddenly minded of the TV comedy *Bottom*, starring Ade Edmondson and Rik Mayall, and the bit when Eddie mistakenly thinks his flatmate Ritchie has topped himself. His stirring epitaph to Ritchie was something to the effect of "Poor blighter. All he needed was the love of a good woman. Well, not even a good one; any old one would have done. Now he's gone and done himself in.") An integral part of the adventure ahead was also the mouth-watering prospect of joining the university mountaineering club and getting among the hills and mountains of Wales and beyond.

Inland from Aberystwyth are the beautiful hills and valleys of central Wales: a place of "hidden hamlets with unpronounceable names, of deeply-cut valleys, thick with hanging oak-woods, of whalebacked hills and grassy sheepwalks" (Kenneth Richmond, quoted in Cocker and Mabey, 2005). As we were winding our way along a road that crested the top of the valley deep below, we saw a bird that was at the time still associated almost exclusively with the rolling hills and wooded valleys of central Wales: the Red Kite. Nowadays you are almost guaranteed to see these birds if you simply drive along the M40; if you turn off and head through the Chilterns you will be inundated with them. Back in 1991, the various reintroduction projects, which eventually led to a population boom, were still in their infancy, and the Red Kite was then a much sought-after bird. We hurriedly ejected ourselves from the car to get better views of this magnificent creature, hanging effortlessly in the air over the steep valley below us. I'd have given my right arm for such a sighting in my birding days proper, when the Red Kite was extremely rare, and when such a spectacle would have been ornithological gold dust. During the following three years at Aberystwyth, I saw many such kites – once rather obligingly drifting over the village in which I lived, hanging in the gentle wind. But they have never lost the power to thrill, especially against the beautiful backdrop of the wooded hills and valleys of central Wales.

My time in Wales also produced a chance sighting of another rare British bird: the Chough. I happened upon a small flock of birds on one of the coastal hills just outside Aberystwyth itself. I knew these birds were very rare and that small numbers occurred in Wales but had no idea I would stumble upon them as I was just ambling about on my own one day. Although I only caught a brief glimpse before they hitched a ride on the wind and tumbled further down the hillside, out of sight, there was no mistaking their identity, with their shiny ink-black plumage and characteristic bright-red legs and bill.

Another time I was watching a group of Jackdaws on such coastal hills, tumbling about like rag dolls in the wind. I then caught sight of a large falcon that, as if waiting until it had my full attention, tucked back its wings and tore through the air in a spectacular dive-bomb, right towards one of the Jackdaws. There was certainly no question as to this bird's identity – it was none other than a Peregrine. The Jackdaw was lucky as it managed to avoid being taken in mid-air by this powerful winged killing machine. The Peregrine, having missed its target, peeled off in flight and then sailed off, probably to try its luck elsewhere.

Although I no longer specifically went birding I still had a strong interest in wildlife, and so, when my housemate invited me on a coach trip to the nature reserve Island of Skomer, off the beautiful Pembrokeshire coast in South Wales, I jumped at the chance. After a predictably stuffy coach journey, we clambered aboard the rather precarious-looking boat and chugged out to sea. As we approached the shallow cliffs of Skomer, a flurry of Puffins filled the skies, with bird after bird cascading down upon the surface of the water, like a winter blizzard. I had only seen one Puffin previously, quite a way out to sea, in its somewhat duller winter plumage. The birds before me now were resplendent, with their characteristic multi-coloured bills, and proudly decked out in their elegant, dinner-jacketed finery. I was surprised at how small they were and even more surprised when, once on the island, they were happy to let me stand so close that I could almost reach over and pick one up. It was certainly tempting, though, despite their inherent cuteness I would likely have lost a finger for my trouble, cleanly snipped off by that formidable bill. Against a backdrop of noisy Kittiwakes, peppered along the cliffs below like a heavy dusting of snow, these Puffins on sentry duty outside their rabbit-burrow-nests were certainly a sight to behold and certainly well worth the journey.

The journey was made even more worthwhile by the sight of a pale-brown bird in low quartering flight over the grassy plain in the centre of the island: a magnificent Short-eared Owl. I was familiar with Short-eared Owls from my early birding years, especially the one we saw at Fobbing marshes amid our river-crossing antics. But there is always something special about these birds with their combination of grace and menace, and the

Island of Skomer – with its screaming seabird colonies and vast stretches of open sea beyond – is surely as good a place as any to watch such a magical hunter.

My university years also furnished me with my first and only taste of continental birding. On a geography field trip to north-eastern Spain, our first port of call amid the sprawling desert-like wastes was the town of Jaca. It was here that, while walking through the streets one evening, on our way to the local bar, I heard a piercing, repetitive yelping noise coming from the branches of a nearby tree. I crept as close as I could until the source of the noise became apparent. It was a tiny greyish owl with small ear tufts and a very fierce expression, glaring at me with its wings held flat against its body in classic alarm pose. It reminded me of a miniature Long-eared Owl that had been painted the wrong colour, though it was not until I returned to the UK and checked my field guide that I was able to put a name to it: Scops Owl. I felt quite privileged to have snatched a glimpse of this beautiful creature sat in a tree in a busy Spanish town, yelping away for all the world to hear (oh how I would *love* to see a vagrant Scops Owl in the UK…). Contrary to 'sod's law', which seems to apply to me without mercy at every juncture, my lack of binoculars did not prevent me from obtaining excellent views of this fine bird, nor of Alpine Choughs later in the week up in the snow-capped Pyrenees, near the French border. I was, however, kicking myself when I saw a bird soaring overhead that I thought might have been an Egyptian Vulture…

Back to the hills

During the mid-90s – around 10 years or so after I had first been mesmerised by its primeval beauty – my brother and I made the long pilgrimage back to the Isle of Skye. We went with an old friend of mine from university, who I had met in the mountaineering club. As well as our sense of humour, another thing we had in common was the fact that we were both *very* ordinary climbers and hillwalkers – almost under-achievers compared to some of the wiry athletic types who would scale a 3,000-foot-plus hill as if it was a stroll in the park, or else shin up a 200-foot overhanging sea cliff without even bothering to use a rope. In contrast, we went on trips with the mountaineering club simply because we were drawn to the splendour and adventure of the hills. These outings, to such places as Snowdonia and Glencoe, also provided us with a golden opportunity to have a damn good laugh and to generally mess about and not take anything seriously much to the annoyance of some of the wiry athletic types.

We started our Skye-bound adventure in the glamorous style in which it was to continue – by spending the first night in our sleeping bags in Glasgow bus station. As well as the hard floor making any semblance of comfort impossible, even with the obligatory thin foam mat beneath us, there was also the incessant white-noise from the monstrous industrial machines, blasting the station with jets of water in the early hours of the morning. In addition, there was the ever-present fear of being set upon by a gang of drunken, hard-as-nails Glaswegians with tattoos and unintelligible accents. Apart from this, I had a great night – I don't think I got any sleep at all! With the exception of a few nights later on in the trip, spent in the relative luxury of a backpackers' hostel, we spent a couple of nights under canvas and were promptly eaten alive by midges upon opening the tent in the morning; a few nights in a remote mountain bothy (hut) with no beds, cushions, electricity, toilets or running water; one night on the beach; plus, to top it all, we spent the last night in unashamed luxury, sleeping next to the trolleys outside Safeway in Fort William.

Looking back on this trip, although I'm glad I had the experience, at the time it was often pretty rough and uncomfortable and with seemingly endless hardships and deprivations. Even such simple British pleasures as having a cup of tea were sometimes too much to ask. After a very long and hard walk to the remote mountain bothy, perched on the coast at the foot of the mighty Cullin hills, we gratefully threw our enormous rucksacks to the floor and collapsed in a sweaty heap beside them. We filled the kettle with water from a nearby river and then sat back as it boiled on the stove, resting our aching limbs and looking forward to copious quantities of tea. When we finally took a much-anticipated mouthful it was truly disgusting – we had made the tea with salt water! We were not quite stupid enough to fill the kettle directly from the sea, but we had filled it from a river that flowed directly into the sea, and had not thought to walk upstream a little to ensure the water was fresh. Revolting as our hot salty tea was, this was only the start of the problems.

The mountain bothy was a relatively short walk from the inlet where, on my previous trip to Skye, I had spent that memorable night in a bivvy bag, gazing at the star-laden skies. The bothy was now to be our new home-from-home for a good few days. Although its sturdy bulk provided shelter from the wind and rain, it was somewhat lacking when it came to basic amenities. I think the only luxury it could boast was a table and a couple of rickety wooden benches. There were certainly no beds, nor anything out of which even Ray Mears could fashion one, and there was no electricity, no running water, and most definitely no toilets. We were also in the company of a gang of mad French Hippies, one of whom had no shoes and wandered about barefoot amid even the most fearsome of rocks. We did, however, bring our own toilet roll, and a small garden trowel with which to dig a small pit – I think you get the picture!

One blustery evening, I set off trowel-in-hand to 'do the business'. When I had found a suitable location, far enough away from the bothy (there were no trees for miles), I started to dig. I was quite pleasantly surprised at how easy it was to slice through the soggy wet turf. Then, to my horror, I discovered that there was a reason why it was so easy to dig in this particular spot: I had simply levered away the top layer of turf from someone else's latrine, this turf having been replaced and patted down by the previous 'occupant'. Unacceptable as this was to my sensibilities, it was now beginning to rain, and I really couldn't be bothered to go and find a new location and start digging afresh. So I did the unthinkable: I squatted over the existing latrine, held my nose as best I could, and reassured myself that this would all be over within a few minutes. Others who visit this location will probably take with them fondly cherished memories of the drama and beauty of this wonderfully isolated landscape. I, on the other hand, am left with the rather ignoble memory of the infamous 'latrine incident'.

Our last few nights on Skye were, thankfully, spent in the unashamed luxury of a backpackers' hostel; after all our hardships and deprivations, we felt this was thoroughly deserved. As well as being adorned with beds, toilets, running water and electricity, the hostel – at Dun Flodigarry, on the north-east coast of the island – also had mountain bikes for hire. With the exception of one occasion when we had caught a ride in the postman's van, which doubled as a bus service to the islanders, we had so far walked everywhere, lugging our back-breaking rucksacks with us. We had tried hitching, but nobody wanted to give a lift to three unwashed and unshaven oiks with wild hair and muddy boots – I can't think why! We therefore jumped at the chance of ditching our rucksacks and taking to the open road on two wheels, and duly headed for the village of Uig on the other side of the island. On our travels we happened upon a Black Guillemot, and also the spectacle of a Golden Eagle flying low across a roadside field, slowly flapping its mighty wings and gradually making off into the distance. This bird was a delight to behold, and its close proximity made up for the fact that we didn't have any binoculars with us. I no longer even owned a pair. This was also my first genuine Golden Eagle – any other sightings over the years having been relegated to the 'can't be sure it wasn't a Buzzard' file.

Another highlight was when we cycled up a steep winding road that snaked back and forth through the enormous jumbled rock formations of the Quiraing: classic picture-postcard Skye scenery. When we had made our way up to a high enough point on the hillside and could take no more, we mopped the sweat from our brows and collapsed onto the floor. After getting our breath back and resting a while, and at the same time taking in the panorama of rock and sea around us, we launched off on our bikes and free-wheeled at break-neck speed all the way back down. This, plus the Golden Eagle encounter, at least went some way to making up for all the hardships and deprivations we had suffered earlier in the week.

Snatched opportunities

During the wilderness years, although I didn't actively go out birding, I never lost the sense of wonder when I saw a bird that was new, special or something a bit unexpected. Sometimes this even brought a smile to my face when I desperately needed it. I remember the joy I felt when I saw a couple of Peregrines soaring and mewing over the probation office in Grays in south Essex, where I had the misfortune to be employed at the time. I hated being a probation officer. Quite apart from my paranoia due to the culture of political-correctness-gone-mad that seemed to be inherent in this service, I simply couldn't keep up with the crippling workloads and felt like little more than a hired slave. One lunchtime, running the gauntlet of the unwashed hordes who would sometimes gather at the door, I nipped out of the office to grab a sandwich, and was greeted by the unexpected sight of these birds drifting in the sky over the buildings – as if to remind me that there was more to life than the spirit-crushing 'nine-to-five'. I really envied their freedom. Unlike me, these wonderful creatures were not imprisoned in an office, facing endless paperwork and impossible deadlines but were free to roam the skies as they pleased.

In a desperate bid to free myself from the monstrous workloads, I left the probation service and became a prison officer. I know exactly what you're thinking: out of the frying pan and into the fire – and you'd be right. After my first day on the wings of Chelmsford nick, I lay in bed at night – awash with anxiety and heart pounding – unable to sleep, as a chilling realisation slowly took hold of me and refused to let go: if I upset the wrong person in this place I could quite possibly get assaulted, beaten up or even stabbed. Slowly but surely it also dawned on me that I had made a BIG mistake. I couldn't just resign after two days though, and a week or so later, as I walked in a semi-daze around the prison service training college, still wondering what the hell I'd let myself in for, I saw a small, streaked bird fluttering around by a small group of trees. It was clearly a bird on a mission, and it seemed to be following the same route as it flitted from tree to tree, then disappeared, then came back into view and repeated the same circuit all over again. I crept as close as I could, using any available cover, until I was near enough to be able to identify it – it was a Spotted Flycatcher. Also, from the purposeful way in which the bird moved from tree to tree, I guessed it had a nest nearby and was frantically dashing around in a bid to fill hungry young stomachs.

Although Spotted Flycatchers are not especially rare, they are not that often encountered, and happening upon one in such circumstances was most definitely something of note. It was surely also better than being in the bar with the other new officers in my section – extremely friendly and supportive though some of them were – who were no doubt trying to drink as much as they could, trying to be as crude as possible, or else planning which member of the opposite sex they were going to try and sleep with that night...or quite possibly all of these. Out here alone, watching the flycatcher on its rounds, I was reminded that when life is kicking you when you're down, the simple enjoyment of birds can bring a ray of sunshine.

71

Return from exile

As the Israelites eventually returned to the Promised Land, my own time of wandering in the desert – an exile from the world of birding – could not last forever. The latter part of the wilderness years saw a gradual re-emergence of my interest in birding, and, although I didn't know it at the time, the turning point was a return to the shiniest of jewels in the RSPB's crown, and the scene of my humiliation all those years previously at the hands of my brother…

Minsmere

After two horrendous years of essay-writing, gargantuan paper exercises (otherwise known as NVQs) and endless deadlines, exasperating political-correctness-gone-mad, and what often felt like a merciless programme of indoctrination at the hands of a bunch of extremist left-wing radical-feminist do-gooder lunatics, which made me more right-wing than ever, I had finally qualified as a probation officer. I was now ready to take my place within the giant bureaucratic production line that is the criminal justice system, where I had earned the right to be a form-filling, box-ticking paperwork machine for the probation service. To celebrate my last day of freedom, one cold, rainy and miserable Sunday in October 2003, I went with my brother to Minsmere for the day, just for old times' sake. Armed with an old pair of binoculars that I borrowed from my dad, plus my brother's now antique Bushnell Spacemaster telescope, we sped off along the wet roads, up through Essex and along the twisting country lanes to the beautiful Suffolk coast.

In the eminently quotable film *Withnail and I*, Withnail (played by Richard E. Grant) emerges from the pub, having, in his own words, just got "utterly arseholed". Together with 'I' (played by Paul McGann), he then struts into the Penrith tearooms and, doing his best to hold himself together, says to the somewhat startled woman, "We want cake and tea." In honour of this cinematic masterpiece, any journey to Minsmere – or anywhere for that matter – is woefully incomplete without an obligatory 'cake and tea' stop in the café. So, when we reached Minsmere, and having satiated our desire for food, drink and *Withnail and I* quotes, not to mention a leisurely stroll around the shop, we headed out to the reserve in a bid to remind ourselves of the joys of birding.

We spent most of what was left of the day ambling around the scrape – a shallow lagoon managed for the benefit of the birds – and trudging along the coast, stopping to enjoy the usual cast of waders and wildfowl from the hides. After seeing the ever-exquisite Avocets, and also likely bemoaning the lack of anything much else bird-wise, we headed back inland for what would undoubtedly be the highlight of the day: the Marsh Harriers patrolling over the reed-beds. After some tantalising glimpses of these once extremely rare birds, we continued along the footpath, through the woods, and then ascended the steps of the 'Bittern hide' to claim our grandstand seat. The Marsh Harriers did not disappoint and danced menacingly over the reeds in full view, as if they were well aware they were under a contractual obligation to perform for the paying visitors.

The rain continued to fall. As the skies grew ever more overcast and the day was starting to draw to a close, we spotted a white bird gracefully but purposefully floating low over the distant fields. It was none other than a Barn Owl hunting, and we eagerly took turns leering through the telescope. Just as we thought this beautiful bird had rounded off the day nicely, and we contemplated going home, my brother suddenly let out a cry of "Bittern!" I quickly lifted my bins and, to my great satisfaction, managed to lock on to this large tawny-brown bird flying low over the reed-bed, its legs trailing behind it in characteristic heron-like fashion. I followed it with my straining eyes until, a few seconds later, it dropped down into the reeds in the last throes of daylight. Yes, I had finally seen my first Bittern. These birds are not only very rare, they are also extremely elusive and notoriously difficult to see, and I had always assumed that I'd never actually be lucky enough to clap eyes on one. But now, after all these years, I had finally seen one, and the warm glow of satisfaction stayed with me all the way home.

Some months later, my brother and I returned to Minsmere, armed with my very own binoculars: a pair that I bought via eBay for about £40, the first ones I had owned in nearly 20 years. Upon arrival at Minsmere, the car park was somewhat full to say the least, and we soon learned that this was because a rarity – a Slender-billed Curlew – had decided to grace the reserve with its presence. We later learned that this was an extremely rare bird – a 'mega-rarity' in the jargonised language of the birding fraternity. We didn't especially intend to chase after the curlew as we were still largely here for old times' sake, though on our usual rounds we did stop in at the north hide to see if another rarity – a Baird's Sandpiper – was still around. It was indeed, but only with the help of a 'proper' birder were we able to find and identify it among the ranks of more familiar-looking waders – not that this bird really stood out at all – bloody waders. Once we had feasted our eyes on this rare, if rather drab-looking bird, we trudged off along the shingle in the direction of the footpath leading to the Bittern hide.

At the start of the footpath, just past the sluice gates, we saw a long line of birders heading off across the field in an altogether different direction; we concluded that they must be after the Slender-billed Curlew. We decided to give it a go. After a short walk we reached the characteristic huddle of blokes with serious expressions and about a million quid's worth of optical and photographic equipment between them. Nobody seemed to be looking through their expensive telescopes (scopes) though, and upon arrival we were told that the bird was last seen about half an hour ago. We decided to wait for a while, during which time more and more birders continued to arrive. As well as learning that some top birders from the continent appeared to be present, it also became apparent that there was some controversy as to whether the bird was in fact a Slender-billed Curlew at all. Despite being surrounded by the elite of the birding world, including the long-bearded, sandal-wearing 'Messiah' himself, none other than the legendary Mr. Bryan Bland, we decided that we couldn't spend our whole afternoon waiting for a bird that might not even put in an appearance and that might not even be a rarity in the first place. So we headed back across the field, past the ranks of birders that were still rushing to the scrum, and along the footpath to the hides.

Also on this day, from one of the hides overlooking the scrape, I caught a glimpse of a lone Red-breasted Goose as it wended its way down onto the water amid a small skein of more familiar-looking geese that had just descended from the skies. Red-breasted Geese are very rare, and I was understandably quite pleased with myself. The only problem with such birds is that you can never be sure they haven't just escaped from a wildfowl collection. Any lingering feelings of pride associated with this sighting have long since been extinguished by the subsequent realisation that, if I'm being entirely honest with myself, in all likelihood it probably was an escapee after all – bloody wildfowl! Anyway, after a cursory perusal of the inhabitants of the scrape, we left the hide and continued on our merry way, heading through the woods and up the steps to the sanctuary of the Bittern hide. Despite much craning of our necks and straining through our bins and scope, we did not see a Bittern flying nervously over the reeds, nor a crisp white Barn Owl hunting over the distant fields – the damn twitchers had probably scared them all away.

Titchwell

Second only in renown to Minsmere among the various RSPB

reserves, Titchwell, on the north Norfolk coast, was our destination for another day's birding – again, just for old times' sake. Almost as soon as we arrived, on the path leading from the car park to the shop, we saw a small huddle of birders staring in the direction of the treetops. After much jockeying and straining through our bins, we eventually saw the birds causing all the commotion: a Lesser Redpoll, a Mealy Redpoll and an Arctic Redpoll. Three new birds within the space of three minutes – not bad going! Unfortunately, I have since learned (courtesy of *Birdguides, 2004)* that the Lesser Redpoll is what was once referred to in the UK as a Common Redpoll, and that the Mealy Redpoll is a different, continental species that is now referred to as a Common Redpoll. And as if that wasn't bad enough, it appears that the term 'Mealy Redpoll' is also now used to refer to the northern race of the Common Redpoll. Confused? Join the club! All is not lost though, as the Arctic Redpoll seems to have escaped this ornithological wrangling, and is still, as far as I can tell, a bona fide rarity. We mere mortals didn't have a hope in hell of differentiating between the birds in the treetops on this particular day, all of which looked identical to me. But with help from some of the birders present, I did at least manage to clap eyes on all three of them. And, as if it goes without saying, one of the birders in the huddle had a very long beard, and is known for his be-smocked sandal-wearing tendencies…

In addition to the flurry of Redpolls and the rubbing of shoulders with the legendary Mr. Bland, this day at Titchwell was also memorable for another reason: I bought myself a brand-new scope and tripod. Among the dizzying array of top-level optics on display in the RSPB shop, the particular model in question– a Nikon spotting scope – was quite modest; its price tag of £350, together with a tripod thrown in for good measure, would not break the bank, unlike some of the other scopes for which you needed to either take out a mortgage or else rob a bank. Handing over three hundred-and-fifty quid is never easy though, and as soon as I parted company with my debit card I wondered if I'd done the right thing. As the birding bug was still only in the process of merely tenderising my flesh, having yet to fully sink its fangs in, I feared I would not get enough use out of the scope to justify such an extravagant outlay. My brother also now had a young daughter, and I feared that opportunities for such sibling birding trips would be few and far between. I didn't especially relish the thought of going birding all on my lonesome. Against these doubts and fears, I reasoned that I was always going to be interested in birds and wildlife, even if I was not into birding in the way that I once was, and that such a purchase should therefore be seen as an investment. Momentarily putting all such thoughts aside, I dumped the boxes and packaging back at the car, set up my new scope and tripod and headed back onto the reserve, proudly holding them aloft for all to see. The much hoped-for influx of roosting winter harriers failed to materialise, and the saving glamour of a Merlin was very much absent too. Our expectation of roosting harriers was, in retrospect, probably quite misplaced. However, the very welcome sight of a ghostly white Barn Owl, hunting in the field right in front of one of the hides, made up for any lack of raptors and was a wonderful bird with which to christen my new scope.

We went on another day trip to Titchwell around this time and happened upon 'Sammy', the resident Black-winged Stilt. Sammy had become something of a celebrity, even having his own range of personalised products on sale in the reserve shop. Although we were unaware of Sammy's celebrity, his rarity status was not lost on us. We watched with delight as he tiptoed delicately through the shallow water at such close quarters that we barely even needed our bins. Unfortunately, there is a sad postscript to this story, as the next time I visited Titchwell I learned that he was missing, presumed dead. Poor Sammy!

As if Sammy the stilt wasn't enough, we also happened upon another celebrity when we paused on the beach for a spot of seawatching. This time there was no characteristic black-and-white body, no long bright-red legs and no delicate prodding of the water with a long needle-like bill. Instead, there was a characteristic long grey beard and... yes, you've guessed it! I'd just like to point out that neither of us were, nor have we ever, been guilty of stalking Mr. Bland. Worshipping from afar wasn't going to be sufficient on this occasion, and when I heard him mention Velvet Scoters out to sea, I couldn't resist the urge to nervously approach in the hope of bagging myself a new bird courtesy of the great man. He was as obliging as ever and very kindly let me have a peak through his scope. He even gave me a quick master class on distinguishing Velvet Scoters among a flock of Common Scoters, a master class from the master himself! Not wishing to outstay my welcome, I retreated sheepishly from his hallowed presence and slithered back to my lowly position with the birding plebs, i.e. my brother. When I had recovered my composure, we feasted our eyes upon the newly-found Velvet Scoters and also enjoyed watching a lovely male Goldeneye close inshore.

Flushed with the success of these recent birding trips, and, with the old birding bug biting ever more ferociously at my heels, I started to feel the need for some half-decent bins to go with my new scope. I had become pretty disillusioned with the bins I had begged and borrowed up to that point, not to mention with those I had recently bought myself, which, in my optical inexperience, I had presumed to be a good set of optics. With all these bins I noticed that, no matter how much I wiped the lenses clean, they always seemed to mist up if there was even a hint of drizzle in the air. On one occasion at Minsmere, among the assembled families in one of the hides, my exact words, spoken just that little bit too loudly, were something to the effect of, "These binoculars are shit!" I subsequently learned that the reason why they kept misting up was that they were not waterproof, and that if you wanted really good bins, you damn well had to pay for them. So one fine day, armed with a nice fat wallet, I headed down to my local Essex Wildlife Trust shop to get to grips with the assembled optics. After much deliberation, and fiddling about with focus wheels and twist-up eyecups, I treated myself to a pair of Opticron roof prism binoculars for £220. I now looked and felt the part, and was ready to hit the birding spots.

Mayday Farm: Operation Goshawk

With precise directions courtesy of the Internet, one spring morning, my brother and I headed off to Mayday Farm near Thetford, in search of what is arguably Britain's most enigmatic and elusive raptor: the Goshawk. Although nothing is guaranteed when it comes to such a secretive bird, the presence of a hide at this site gave me a level of confidence that was, as I later found out, hopelessly misplaced. Upon arrival at the site, we learned from another birder that a Goshawk had been seen that morning. We raced off to the hide, took our grandstand seats and waited for the performance to start. We waited…and waited…and waited. Slowly it dawned on us that the only birds we were going to see from this hide were Chaffinches. When we had finally had enough and thought our joints were going to seize up, we quietly left the hide and started on a circuit of the forest rides, keeping a careful watch for the slightest movement in the trees, or the merest hint of a silhouette against the bright sunny skies. Despite our best efforts, we saw nothing more exciting than a couple of crows taunting us over the treetops, and eventually decided that we really couldn't be bothered anymore. We walked back to the car with our tails between our legs and headed home dejectedly.

I was not going to give up that easily though. Not long after our initial aborted mission, one fine Saturday morning saw me heading eagerly up the A14 – this time alone – in a bid to be in prime position as early as possible. Although I don't think I even bothered going in the hide this time probably for fear of discovering the cobwebbed skeletons of other birders who had long since died of boredom, I did have a good scan around above the treetops. I continued walking along the winding path, deeper and deeper into the forest. I went past a dilapidated abode that housed either a wicked witch, or else a daddy bear, a mummy bear and a baby bear, until I came to a large open space that had only recently been felled of its trees. As I sat down for a rest, and tea from my flask, I saw two fairly large and remarkably hawk-like birds over the treetops in the middle distance. I rapidly set up my scope and tripod, though by the time I was ready to roll they had disappeared from view – typical! I quickly made my way across the open ground to the edge of the forest beyond and started scouting out the area. Soon I saw a fairly large raptor gliding across the treetops, steadily losing height as it cut through the air, whereupon it disappeared into the forest. This bird too was remarkably hawk-like, and its fairly large size led me to the tantalising conclusion that it must have been a Goshawk. Dare I believe it though? I paced up and down in a state of agitation, anxiously waiting for another sighting that would clinch it. After a nervous wait, I again caught sight of a largish hawk over the treetops, this time turning in a tight circle with its tail spread out like a fan. My trusted field guide confirmed that Goshawks have rounded tail corners compared to the sharp tail corners of a Sparrowhawk. Shortly after this, I saw another very large-looking hawk of a dull-brownish colour; these birds simply had to be Goshawks. Finally I had seen a Goshawk!

As well as being both scarce and extremely elusive, Goshawks also have a fierce and menacing glamour that, at least to my mind, outdoes even that of top aerial performers like the Peregrine. What an amazing bird, and also one that my brother has yet to see. I lost no time at all in sending him a text, informing him of the good news – in capital letters, of course, and followed by several exclamation marks.

I basked in the happiness of my Goshawk sighting for a good couple of weeks until, slowly but surely, the old nagging conscience started to kick in. How could I be 100% sure they were not female Sparrowhawks, female Sparrowhawks being of a similar size to male Goshawks? I reminded myself of the rounded tail corners, and tried to convince myself that I was just being neurotic. Much as I tried to repress these doubts, they came flooding to the surface a few months later when I was at the raptor watchpoint at Great Ryburgh in Norfolk, one of the best places in the UK to see the rare Honey Buzzard. There I overheard a seasoned birder, who was also a member of the local Honey Buzzard monitoring group, talking about how inexperienced birders come to Great Ryburgh and convince themselves that they have seen Honey Buzzards, when they have in fact merely been duped by the superficially very similar Common Buzzard. He went on to describe how such folk are also similarly duped by large Sparrowhawks while seeking out Goshawks at Mayday Farm, and stated in no uncertain terms that, when you actually do see a Goshawk for the first time, you damn well know you've seen one.

The awful truth was staring me in the face, and I couldn't ignore it a moment longer: there was no way I could be sure the birds I had seen were not female Sparrowhawks. I therefore reluctantly but dutifully removed the mental tick that I had placed next to the word 'Goshawk' in my mind. As with the bitterest case of unrequited love, and the moment that all one's cherished hopes and desires crumble, I mentally hung my head in embarrassed shame and bid a sad farewell to the misplaced euphoria that had all been for nothing.

Minsmere revisited

Despite now being a veteran of lone stakeouts deep in the forest in search of elusive Goshawks, I still did not especially relish the idea of birding alone. So one clear summer's day, with the promise of lovely surroundings and the obligatory *Withnail and*

I-esque 'cake and tea' stop in the café, I persuaded some of my friends to accompany me on a day's birding trip to Minsmere. They were most definitely non-birders, although Panda (because it rhymes with Amanda – very original!) was quite interested in wildlife, gardening and horticulture, and is on record as saying that if she were a bit older she could quite fancy Alan Titchmarsh. This was in the days when Alan Titchmarsh was still primarily known as a gardener; now it feels like his face is everywhere, even – rather inappropriately in my view – fronting major BBC series on wildlife and natural history. Bear (because it rhymes with Clare) was the designated driver and dutifully drove us up the A12, through the winding country lanes and all the way to Minsmere. After the requisite lunch stop in the café, we headed out to the reserve to do the rounds.

In the company of such novices, I felt like a birding expert conducting a guided tour. My own birding experience was also enhanced somewhat, as I was forced to take note of and explain the diagnostic features of the more common birds. Had I been on my own or with my brother, I would more than likely have turned my nose up at these birds, and I was, quite rightly, accused of being a bird snob on more than one occasion throughout the day. Panda in particular gained full marks for her birding enthusiasm, even if she did lose points later in the day for saying sarcastically, "There's a Turkey", directly in the hearing of other birders. She did, however, cop a well-deserved comedy beating for such outrageous behaviour!

The Avocets were as graceful as ever on the scrape, a Great Spotted Woodpecker shinned up a tree in the woods and the Marsh Harriers were well and truly on form over the reed-bed from the Bittern hide. One of the Marsh Harriers caused much panic-stricken squealing among the baby Coots as it plunged into the reeds with its talons outstretched, though to our great relief they lived to tell the tale. Impressive as the Marsh Harriers were, the undoubted stars were the Hobbies that periodically streaked across the reeds immediately in front of the hide. They were clearly aware of the host of onlookers in need of entertainment, as during their spectacular fly-pasts they would twist and turn obligingly in mid-air, giving the appreciative crowd a flash of their dashing red trousers. One of these fine birds was even kind enough to perch on a fence-post for a while, affording us wonderful views through the scope.

Hobbies are always a joy to behold, and I had not set eyes on one of these impressive beasts since our trip to Thursley Common all those years before. As we gazed out of the Bittern hide in awe of the aerial performance, I couldn't resist letting out a cry of, "Red trousers...incoming...from the right," in my best RAF wing commander accent. Amid such foolery I also managed to catch glimpses of two – yes, two – Bitterns flying low over the reeds. Much to my disappointment, none of my friends managed to see either bird. Oh well, seeing a Bittern – let alone two – on your first trip to Minsmere would be just a bit too jammy; let them work for their Bitterns like I had to.

Minsmere still had another trick up its sleeve though; on the way back from the Island Mere Hide we happened upon a sight that I don't think any of us had ever seen before, and probably never will again. I had grown accustomed to being pleasantly surprised by the doe-eyed Muntjac Deer creeping through the undergrowth at Minsmere, though none of us expected to see what lay just a few feet away to the left of the track: the cutest little Badger cub you could possibly imagine! It seemed totally oblivious to us, and amid much admiration and hushed exclamations of "Aaaah!" I cautiously crept to within about two feet of it, posing for Panda who slowly unleashed her camera and started snapping away. I was so close to this delightful little chap that I could have stroked it. But as well as possibly having my fingers bitten, I didn't want to run the risk of it smelling of humans and being abandoned by its mother. So we slowly retreated, leaving the cub to continue sniffing around the vegetation, completely unaware that this blessed encounter had well and truly made our day.

Norfolk: summer raptor quest

There was no stopping me now, and later in the summer my brother and I set off to Norfolk for the day in a bid to see the rare and elusive Honey Buzzard. We left obscenely early in the morning, arriving at Fakenham before most of the shops had opened. After a spot of breakfast and a pot of tea, we headed off through the winding country roads to the raptor watchpoint at Great Ryburgh.

The place seemed promising enough, as almost immediately upon arrival we saw a Marsh Harrier patrolling low over the arable fields on the horizon. However, after much neck-craning and eye-straining there was still no sign of a Honey Buzzard, though we did see the odd Hobby tearing across the sky. We also gained some valuable 'gen' (information on the whereabouts of a bird) in the form of precise directions to the nest site of the extremely rare Montagu's Harrier, the Internet birding community quite rightly being unwilling to make public such information. So we jumped in the car and set off along the narrow roads that wound their way through the arable fields and tiny villages of Norfolk.

Upon arrival at the site, and to my great surprise and joy, I spotted a couple of harriers flying low over the field and set up the scope and tripod with all the speed that my clumsy fingers could muster. I should have known that such a scarce quarry would not present itself so easily, and soon learned that these birds were Marsh Harriers. I also learned of the ominous news that every birder dreads upon arrival at a birding site: the Montagu's Harriers were not currently showing, but were seen earlier this morning – typical. I watched the Marsh Harriers in my scope for a while, wishing that they would somehow morph into a 'Monty's'.

Despite the growing sinking feeling in my stomach, our patience was soon rewarded as a sudden shout indicated that the Monty's was back. I raised my bins to secure the much-anticipated sighting, then frantically located the bird in my scope and clung on to it for dear life as it drifted brazenly across the arable fields, in full view of the appreciative crowd. Fate was clearly on our side, as, rather than a drab female or juvenile bird, this was none other than a beautiful male in all its silver glory. It quickly became apparent how different this species is from the superficially similar, though considerably bulkier, Hen Harrier; this slim and elegant creature flew with such delicate grace that the description of its flight in the Collins field guide (2001) as "buoyant and tern-like" seemed almost to be an understatement. The views obtained in the scope were positively to die for, and I even noted some of the finer diagnostic plumage details.

All good things must come to an end, however, and having wooed the grateful crowd with its abundant charms, this beautiful silver vision eventually dropped down into the crops and out of view. Although we waited around for an encore, this stunning bird had already given a star performance well beyond the call of duty, so we headed back to Great Ryburgh to see if we could round off the day nicely with a Honey Buzzard. The 'Honeys' were clearly in no mood to oblige, not even with a distant glimpse, and after a while we became bored of watching the empty skies. It had been a long and tiring day, and so we stretched out on our backs amid the stunted hedgerow, closed our eyes and drifted off to sleep.

I returned to Great Ryburgh again that summer, this time on my own. The Honey Buzzards continued to elude me, though a trip to the Montagu's Harrier site did produce views of a juvenile bird, perched on the hedge on the far side of the field. It was not the greatest of views, resembling more of a distant brown blob rather than a bird, though the other birders present assured me that it was indeed a Monty's. I waited around in the hope that one of the adult birds would drop by to feed it, but it was not to be on this occasion. Although something of an anti-climax compared to the previous sighting, it was still a Monty's, and I left with a feeling of achievement nonetheless.

It was also on this day that I went to the RSPB reserve at Lakenheath in a bid to see Golden Orioles, an extremely rare breeding bird. I made the mistake of following the footpath all the way around the reserve with my legs clad only in shorts, and was led a not-so-merry dance through vast swathes of waste-high stinging nettles; needless to say, my legs ended up somewhat red and blotchy…feeling as if millions of invisible ants were feasting on them. Although it almost goes without saying, I failed to secure even the merest hint of a Golden Oriole. At Weeting Heath I did manage to clap eyes on a Stone Curlew – just about. The view was even worse than that of the juvenile Monty's, and to my eyes was little more than a distant and inanimate speck high on the shimmering hillside. Instead of sitting in front of the hides like it's supposed to, this bird thought it would have a bit of a laugh at our expense by taking itself up on to the hillside way behind the reserve. I was, however, assured by the teenager working in the information centre that the distant speck was, in fact, a genuine Stone Curlew. Although the views were nowhere near as good as I'd have liked, I suppose a Monty's and a Stone Curlew is not bad for a day's birding.

A match made in Norfolk

Day tripping

In the summer of 2005, I went to Norfolk for the day with Panda – one of the friends who had previously accompanied me to Minsmere on the 'baby Badger' day. We arrived at the Great Ryburgh raptor watchpoint at about 8.15am. This was pretty good going, especially considering the long journey, and also the fact that we had only narrowly avoided a head-on collision with an oncoming lorry on the narrow country roads. Despite our prompt arrival, the Honey Buzzards were still nowhere to be seen, though we did see a very strange-looking goose-like bird, which prompted quite a buzz and we hurriedly flicked through the pages of my field guide.

Despite my initial excitement that I may have seen a stray Ruddy Shelduck – an extremely rare bird – I soon learned that it was an Egyptian Goose. It was part of the local feral population of this non-native species, and we soon located an entire flock of them feeding in the adjacent field. As well as being quite special, not to mention rather attractive, this was also a new bird for both of us. Having enjoyed the Egyptian Geese and cursed the skies for their omnipresent lack of 'Honeys', we got in the car and made our way to the raptor watchpoint at Swanton Novers to try our luck there. The Honeys were still not playing ball, so we headed off to Morston to book ourselves on a boat trip to see the seals on Blakeney Point, and then to Titchwell to enjoy a stilton and mushroom baguette – and the obligatory cup of tea and stroll around the shop.

There was not an awful lot to write home about at Titchwell, though I did manage to see my first Mediterranean Gull – courtesy of one of the RSPB staff in the hide, who kindly pointed out its diagnostic features. It's a good job he did, as in my desire to impress Panda with something special (or 'bird-snobbery' as she called it), I hadn't even bothered to look at the usual cast of gulls, waders and wildfowl. There were also Curlew Sandpipers present, though as I was under the very much mistaken impression that they were of no more interest than the assembled Dunlin and Knot, I only paid them scant attention. In a classic case of poetic justice, I have recently concluded that, in all likelihood, I didn't even see the Curlew Sandpipers on this day. As I assumed that I had already seen them when perusing the wader flocks, I didn't even bother to locate them and look at them properly, though what I had been looking at were probably Dunlins. Now I'm not sure if I've ever seen a Curlew Sandpiper, and I have been forced to strike the bird from my list of sightings. Anyway, we headed down to the beach for a spot of seawatching, where we saw some small dark blobs – otherwise known as Common Scoters – passing by, though not an awful lot else. The clock was now ticking very rapidly indeed, and having sampled the delights of Titchwell, we hastily made our way through the deserted country roads in order to make it in time for the boat trip to see the seals.

We stopped only to rescue a rather myxomitosed rabbit from the road, hoping that the poor creature would be afforded a quick and pain-free death, and eventually lurched into Morston harbour with about one minute to spare. Having parked the car and joined the queue for the boat, I was given a firm kick up the backside courtesy of Sod's Law, in the form of a sudden and overwhelming urge to empty my bladder. Torn between the choice of an agonizing cross-legged boat trip or blessed relief, I opted for the latter. I ran for all I was worth to the distant toilet block and then sprinted back in a desperate bid to avoid missing the boat. I was also quite keen not to incur the wrath of Panda, which I now know outdoes even that of the Lord in the Old Testament when He's none-too-pleased with the children of Israel! By some kind of miracle, I managed to just about make it in time, and, gasping for breath amid desperate asthmatic wheezes, I took my place on the boat and settled back to enjoy.

The boat trip was worth every penny, not to mention the trauma involved in our desperate bid to make it on time, as we were treated to spectacular views of both Common and Grey Seals. Hauled up rather awkwardly on the sand, the seals eyed us with their characteristic laid-back curiosity as we passed gently by. At times we pulled up so close alongside them that I thought some were going to try and hitch a ride, though it did enable Panda to get some cracking photos. She also managed to film a short moving sequence of the seals on her camera, during which I can quite clearly be heard asking her if, like the seals, she would like to be the proud owner of a pair of flippers instead of feet; she said she would, though she really shouldn't encourage me!

After our wonderful close encounter with the seals, we headed off to Cley, trying to forget that our day was drawing to a close, and that we'd soon have to head for home. We parked in the beachfront car park and trudged through the energy-sapping, spirit-crushing shingle to the nearest hide. By the time we hoisted up the shutters and looked out on what appeared to be a birdless expanse of mud and grass, I had finally given up on seeing anything special, and now pinned all my hopes on a last-minute Barn Owl to save the day. Unfortunately it was not to be, and we duly headed off into the village of Cley-next-the-Sea for a late lunch. This was our second lunch of the day; we enjoyed houmous in pitta bread while perched on a veranda, overlooking the coastal reed-beds in the late afternoon sunshine. Although this was close to being a perfect way to round off the day, we felt that things were not really complete without an obligatory stop for a pizza once we arrived back in Essex.

Mini-break: birding and bishops

As Panda had really enjoyed our day in Norfolk, and as I now had a bona fide birding partner, one early morning in late September we headed off again. This time we had the unashamed luxury of four whole days of birding to look forward to, and started the day in style with a quality breakfast in the town of Swaffham, en-route, once again, to the north Norfolk coast.

Our Bed and Breakfast was in the tiny and rather isolated village of Walsingham. Unbeknown to us at the time, Walsingham is a major centre for Christian pilgrimage, boasting as it does both an Anglican and a Catholic shrine – it is not for nothing that Walsingham is known as 'England's Nazareth'. There are also at least two Orthodox chapels and a host of shops selling everything from incense to vicars' robes, innumerable crucifixes and wooden icons, and a whole range of books on everything to do with Christ, Christianity and 'the Church'. In addition to birding and wildlife, my other major interest is in spirituality, meditation and contemplative prayer – or 'monkery' as we know it for short – as in what monks do, so in between bouts of birding I simply couldn't get enough of this place. We had also caught the tail end of pilgrim season, which meant that the streets were buzzing, not only with pilgrims who had come from far and wide to pay homage to the shrines of 'Our Lady of Walsingham', but also with vicars, nuns, reverends, bishops and archbishops, all decked out in their flowing robes and white-collared regalia. It was quite surreal; we felt as if we had inadvertently wandered onto the set of Channel 4's *Father Ted*. Anyway, as Ted's fellow priest Father Jack would say when he could manage to prise his mouth away from the whisky bottle for more than two seconds – "That would be an ecumenical matter."

Our first birding port of call was Titchwell, where we saw a dainty Red-necked Phalarope, feeding frantically in the shallow lagoon with its needle-sharp bill. Its non-stop pirouetting motion gave it all the grace of a ballet dancer. After savouring this rather lovely spectacle we headed to the beach to engage in some autumn seawatching. We managed to see a Great Skua patrolling along the shore, and a Red-throated Diver and Red-necked Grebe out to sea, the latter being a new bird for me. Courtesy of the very obliging birder who helped us find these birds, we also learned of the presence of a Red-backed Shrike at Friary Hills, near Blakeney harbour, and a Spotted Crake at Kelling. We also heard, via a very helpful pager-toting member of staff in the RSPB shop at Titchwell, of a Yellow-browed

Warbler at Holkham pines.

Despite much frenzied searching and scurrying at Friary Hills, the shrike was nowhere to be seen. At Kelling, after scampering down a muddy footpath, we did manage to get extremely good views of the Spotted Crake as it periodically emerged from the reeds to feed at the water's edge. This was another new bird, plus we also got some good views of a couple of tiny Little Stints. The Yellow-browed Warbler would prove to be somewhat more challenging, and my initial attempt at 'poaching', i.e. casually walking up to the nearest tripod-toting *Homo sapiens* in the hope that they had just seen it, proved to be unsuccessful. As I should have known, locating the bird among the massed ranks of pine trees turned out to be about as difficult as trying to find a microscopic needle amid a gathering of gargantuan haystacks. The RSPB warden at Titchwell told us to look for a tit flock and then listen out for the Yellow-browed's characteristic call, though as you may not be surprised to know, I didn't even have the faintest idea what this sounded like. The warden even very obligingly played us a short audio sample of the call, though by the time we hit the footpath at Holkham Pines, all trace of it had managed to fully vacate my brain cells; we didn't stand a chance. Still, Holkham Pines is a very beautiful place, and, as if to remind us that chasing after rarities is not the be-all and end-all, a scythe-winged Hobby flashed majestically across the treetops and headed off into the dazzling sunshine. Holkham pines is also perhaps the best place in Norfolk to see wintering Pink-footed Geese; we momentarily enjoyed the spectacle of massed ranks of these creatures grazing amid the vast stretches of tussocky grass.

A trip to Holme, with its beautiful sand dunes, pine trees and wide expanses of glistening wet beaches, unfortunately produced nothing more exciting than a few distant Gannets out to sea. Back at Titchwell, we saw a rather dashing Hobby flying low across the waves close inshore, plus another rarity in the form of a Temminck's Stint back on the lagoon. I wouldn't even have noticed this inconspicuous little wader were it not for another birder who, in response to my rather leading questions, very kindly pointed out both the bird and also its diagnostic features. The act of poaching, as I had come to call it, may not be the most honourable of birding behaviours, though if it means I actually see the bird then I'm all for it. I've even crafted it into an art form, and it has certainly paid off on occasions, sometimes with some quite rare birds. Given that I'm not only a very ordinary and rather mediocre birder, but also quite a lazy one, surely I can't be expected to find *and* identify rare and difficult birds all on my own! As well as my thoroughly shameful poaching activities, Titchwell was also the scene of perhaps my most embarrassing birding moment to date – of which Panda never tires of reminding me.

Having hit the beach to see what was around, I was peering through my scope at the assembled waders on the rocky seashore, when I noticed a bird that, to me anyway, looked quite unusual. A Pectoral Sandpiper – a genuine if minor rarity – had been reported at Titchwell, so I rapidly thumbed through my field guide until I found a picture of it. The picture looked similar to the bird in my scope, though not similar enough for me to be certain. I therefore approached another birder who was standing nearby, informed him that I had a 'possible', and asked him if he could come and confirm it for me. As if on cue, the bird duly disappeared behind the rocks, where it remained hidden – for just about long enough to cause considerable discomfort and embarrassment on my part. Just when the other birder was starting to think I was experiencing rare-wader hallucinations, the bird in question reappeared. I located it in my scope and then turned to the other birder for the verdict that I hoped would vindicate my initial hunch. After clapping eyes on it for all of a second, he delivered the damning verdict: it was a Knot. A Knot?? Aaghh!! I was so busy fixating on rarities that I didn't even know what the common birds looked like! I apologised for the false alarm, hung my head in shame and trudged back to Panda with my tail between my legs – all the while praying that the rocks would suddenly be rent asunder and that I'd be sucked down into a subterranean magma chamber, never again having to show my face in front of other birders. The birder in question – who very kindly reassured me that I should not feel the need to apologise – was a very fine and distinguished chap called Murray. My moment of birding humiliation would thenceforth be forever known as my 'Murray moment'. I've said it before and I'll say it again: bloody waders!

Dungeness

Good old Dungeness was also the focus of our birding activities around this time, though my initial trip there was without my newfound birding partner. Courtesy of the information board at the RSPB reserve, I learned that a Dusky Warbler – quite a rarity – had been seen at the ARC pits, so I headed off to look for the characteristic huddle of birders. Perhaps it was a good thing that this particular feathered chap wasn't playing ball, as I wouldn't have had a hope in hell of distinguishing it from a Chiffchaff or Willow Warbler. I did, however, manage to see my second Baird's Sandpiper from the hide. After heading down to the power station to indulge in some seawatching, I got some cracking views of Arctic Skuas twisting and turning in aerial pursuit of some rather unfortunate terns. More than a year after this trip to Dunge, it came to my attention that, while trying to snatch a glimpse of the Dusky Warbler, I was in the presence of none other than Lee Evans himself – that almost mythical top twitcher and year lister.

On the next trip to Dunge, this time accompanied by Panda, we saw some Slavonian Grebes on the far side of one of the roadside gravel pits. This was a new bird for both of us, though I was also very proud of the fact that I had distinguished them from the very similar – at least in winter plumage – Black-necked Grebe all on my own…well, just me and my field guide anyway. It was not until some weeks later that I realised I had misinterpreted the text in the field guide, mistakenly concluding that a distinguishing feature of the Slavonian Grebe was its white wingbar. I later found out that both these species of grebe have a white wingbar, and realised that, at the distances from which we had viewed them, they would have been totally indistinguishable, at least by me anyway. We didn't see anything else exciting, though did manage to rescue an injured Collared Dove on our way to Rye, just down the coast from Dunge. The poor dove was flailing around in the road, having clearly just been hit by a car. I stopped my car, got out and gently lifted the unfortunate creature from the floor. What to do with it though? I didn't think there was much chance of it surviving, so I placed it in a field, out of immediate harm's way. It was still flopping around though, and I couldn't just leave it. So we drove it back to the RSPB reserve at Dunge, where the young volunteer kindly agreed to take it in and try to contact the local animal hospital. We sincerely hoped the dove would recover, or else have a quick and painless death. We then headed for Rye to sample the delights of the fish and chip restaurant. Food and birds: a winning combination every time!

Targeted strikes

My burgeoning friendship and joint birding activities with Panda had already started to bear fruit in more ways than one, and our trip to Dunge was to be the final culmination of a good few weeks of pretty intense flirting. When we returned from Dunge, my kitchen (well, my parents' actually) became the scene of a rather embarrassing 'fumble', and although this nearly went horribly wrong, it nevertheless marked our official transition from friendship to 'coupledom'. I had assumed that these things became easier the older you got – how wrong I was! With my official birding trophy wife (as she was jokingly called) now in tow, I was raring to go.

A private viewing

Nothing beats a good day out birding in places like north Norfolk. But there can be times when rarities put in an appearance not too far from home, and in such circumstances it would simply be rude not to go and pay homage. A bit like the time when a Grey-cheeked Thrush – an extremely rare American vagrant – was found by chance in a country park in Hertfordshire. I had previously seen a Grey-cheeked Thrush on the Scillies, shortly before it found its way into the jaws of that hungry cat. As this was nearly 20 years before, and as I now had someone special with whom I could share the joys of birding, it was as if I was starting again from scratch. I therefore felt the same anticipation as I had all those years ago when I was trying to see this bird for the first time. So one bitterly cold winter's day, armed with maps and directions courtesy of my new subscription to an online birding information service, we headed off around the M25 and into the depths of the Hertfordshire countryside.

Once at the country park, we hurried along a muddy footpath and were greeted with the news that every birder loves to hear: that the bird was indeed showing. We paced on until we came to the telltale huddle of birders peering into the bushes, then assembled the scope and set about the task of locating our quarry. Despite the initial harbinger of good news, we were now greeted with the news that every birder dreads: it *was* showing, but it isn't anymore!

After spending the best part of an hour staring in vain at the leaf litter and periodically checking the body language of other birders for any signs of a sighting, there was a sudden flurry of activity as news spread that the bird had been relocated. We rushed ahead with the herd and then jostled for position at the new vantage point. The bird was still deep in the undergrowth and proving to be very elusive. After much frantic prolonged staring and straining, all I had seen was the briefest glimpse of its legs as it scurried along a fallen branch in the tangled leaf litter. I was very happy for Panda, as she had managed to catch a glimpse of the bird itself. And while, technically at least, I didn't even 'need' the bird, I nevertheless still felt very disappointed that I had not seen it properly. I stayed put in the hope of one last sighting before we left, though the dusk of an early winter evening was just around the next corner and approaching rapidly. As the light began to fade, and as all traces of activity in the leaf litter seemed to have ceased altogether, one-by-one the assembled birders gradually filed away until only Panda and I were left in the encroaching woodland gloom.

Just as we were about to head off, and in the very last throes of daylight, a small grey bird with a spotted breast emerged from the undergrowth and proceeded to hop fearlessly across the muddy path in front of us, no more than ten feet away. That was it! That was the Grey-cheeked Thrush! We managed to get fantastic views through our bins as it paused momentarily, then continued to hop across the path and on into the leaf litter. We couldn't believe our luck. It was as if it was just waiting for all the other birders to go before it decided to reward our patience with a private viewing, just for us! As if to confirm this, the bird disappeared from view just as another frantic birder arrived in the very last seconds of daylight. Despite our noble attempts to find the thrush for this unfortunate last-minute birder it was not to be, and we trudged back through the muddy darkness, awash with our success.

Supermarket Sweep

Around this time we also learned of a group of scarce and very beautiful winter visitors, virtually on our doorstep. A flock of Waxwings were reported to be frequenting a roundabout next to the Aldi store in Pitsea – a mere stone's throw from Wat Tyler country park. I had seen my very first Waxwings the previous winter at Cheshunt in Hertfordshire, with my brother, where they were plucking the berries from the bushes, just along the high street from Somerfield. I desperately wanted Panda to see these birds, plus it is always a pleasure to watch such strikingly beautiful creatures no matter how many times one may already have seen them.

After our initial failure at the roundabout in question, we drove the short distance to the Tesco car park, where the Waxwings had also been reported (Aldi, Somerfield, Tesco: what is it with Waxwings and supermarkets?!). Upon arrival, I noticed a flock of Starlings high above in the trees, though I thought it would be prudent to check them out in my bins, just to be certain. The characteristic crest of feathers indicated that these were no Starlings; I happily informed Panda that I had found the Waxwings. As we moved closer we also noticed that there were some Waxwings in the bushes at the foot of the trees, so approached with our bins at the ready. Waxwings are rather nervous creatures and don't seem to stay put for long, though before they took flight in the direction of the next sprig of berries, we were at least afforded enough time to savour their winter beauty.

Bloody wildfowl!

On another birding mission around this time, we managed to see a Great Northern Diver, a Black-throated Diver and a Long-tailed Duck – all on the same day. To see both diver species

97

(with fantastic views of the Great Northern) on the same day, and on the same inland lake in Cambridgeshire, miles from the sea…surely this is really quite something. Add to this a short trip to see a beautiful male Long-tailed Duck – which seemed as indifferent to the close attention of humans as any self-respecting garden Robin – and you can see why we were quite pleased with ourselves. We should have made the most of this feeling while we could, as all attempts to round off the day with an American Wigeon – a genuine if minor rarity – on an isolated and rather dingy gravel pit proved utterly fruitless. I think I actually did see the bird in question in the very last moments of daylight, though I was fully reliant on the word of another birder, of whose credentials I could not be certain. And even if technically I had seen the bird, it certainly didn't feel like it. When I see a bird for the first time, not only do I want to be sure of its identification, I also want slightly more than a fleeting glimpse of a distant murky blob. As Panda had also failed to see the bird, I therefore did the honourable thing and discounted the sighting with a mental note to try again on another day when there was slightly more daylight – as we subsequently did, only to fail miserably once again.

If such a near miss was not sufficient to convince us that there was surely more to birding than chasing after rarities, our trip to Chilham Water in Kent to see a Hooded Merganser a few days later surely was. We both saw the bird eventually, however, this was far from easy, given that the surface of the lake was as misty as a lonely medieval moor. The only problem was that, as soon as we started to revel in our sighting, we were informed – by my brother, much to his glee – that we couldn't count it after all. Apparently, the word among the Internet birding community was that it was very likely an escapee, i.e. not a genuine wild bird. It was also a similar story with the Snow Geese we saw later that winter at Dungeness. And I won't even mention the Ferruginous Duck – probably a genuinely wild bird – that we failed to see on something like five different visits to the same fishing lake in a godforsaken corner of Kent. And the Lesser Scaup that we missed out on after travelling all the way to Ouse Washes in Cambridgeshire… I've said it before and I'll say it again: bloody wildfowl! This would also be a good place to whinge about the Ring-billed Gull (named 'Rossi', due to its predilection for hanging around the Rossi ice cream parlour) that we continuously missed, despite it taking up winter residence on a stretch of seashore at Southend-on-Sea – virtually our back garden. This would, however, render totally null and void my nice little heading for this section, and, considering the run-around that 'Rossi' has given us, I'm damned if he's getting a heading all to himself. Bloody gulls!

Good old RSPB

As if to remind us that fate's vast armies are not always conspiring to bring about our birding demise, there is always the odd rarity that proves it's always worth putting in the effort, especially when it's close to home. Such was the case with the Sociable Lapwing at RSPB Rainham Marshes, on the heavily industrialised fringes of East London. Upon arrival, we headed out to the seawall and trudged briskly along the track to the gathered herd of birders. We were duly pointed in the direction of the bird, which was sitting nonchalantly amid the assembled waders. Being as it was in its rather dour winter plumage, this was not the most stunning creature I had ever laid eyes upon. It was, however, an extremely rare bird in the UK, and also (as I understand) quite rare globally. Rainham Marshes was also the scene of another birding coup, this time in the form of a couple of Penduline Tits nibbling on the bulrushes on the fringes of the reserve. Great views were had; unfortunately Panda was not with me on this occasion. The usual warm glow of having successfully caught up with another rarity was therefore somewhat less intense, though, on a cold and windswept day at Rainham Marshes you certainly need all the warmth you can get.

Up close and personal

One of our sweetest birding successes occurred on a day when we were looking for Goshawks at Elveden forest, near Thetford.

99

Morning was drawing to a close, and we had given up all hope of seeing one of these elusive beasts. We did, however, learn of the presence of a Killdeer, a very rare American wader, in Blakeney harbour, on the north Norfolk coast (by all accounts the bird was there for the taking). As we love this part of Norfolk anyway, we decided that trying to see this bird would be a good way to spend the afternoon. After a leisurely drive through the beautiful Norfolk countryside, we rolled into Blakeney harbour and parked the car. We were soon pointed in the direction of the Killdeer and also told the news that we wanted to hear: it was indeed showing. After a blissfully short walk, we came to the characteristic huddle of birders, some 30 feet in front of which was the Killdeer, strutting around on the mud for all to see. It most certainly was there for the taking; the fantastic close-up views made every mile we had travelled more than worth it. Our only regret was that it was Sunday afternoon, and no sooner had we had our fill of the Killdeer than we had to think about the long drive home; oh how we wished we lived in Norfolk.

More than a match for the Killdeer was the Long-billed Dowitcher – another rare American wader – at Oare Marshes in north Kent. On this occasion, we were greeted with the news that the bird had not been seen for around half-an-hour or so, and we sought consolation by trying to convince ourselves that we could get just as much pleasure from looking at the more familiar waders and wildfowl. Despite my best efforts, I simply could not get worked up about Greylag Geese and Snipe, beautiful though the latter was, and thankfully it wasn't long before the dowitcher was relocated. We rushed to get a fix on the bird in the scope, though we needn't have worried, as it soon came even closer to us than had the Killdeer. In the afternoon sunshine we feasted upon the high definition close-up views, which included every detail of its beautiful mottled plumage. If ever there was a bird to slap you in the face with the realisation that even the best paintings by the best artists in the best field guides cannot truly do justice to the intricate beauty of a bird's plumage, then this was it.

As wonderful as both the Killdeer and dowitcher were, the prize for the most memorable targeted strike surely has to go to the Red-backed Shrike we saw one beautiful summer's day on a small tract of scrubland in Hertfordshire. Having missed this bird on our first attempt to see it, we returned the following weekend to give it one last chance. As if to make up for its previous poor show, this bird decided that, on this particular day, it would pull out all the stops and put on the performance of a lifetime. Shortly after we arrived, the bird was duly located amid the branches of the scrub. It then rather obligingly perched brazenly on the outer branches, no more than 30 feet or so away from our eager gaze. Its bold and handsome plumage was resplendent in the glorious heat of the late summer sunshine; and the views through the scope were simply to die for. Although technically not a new bird for me, the only other Red-backed Shrike I had seen was more than 20 years earlier, and any memory of this sighting was now a very distant blur. As well as being exceptionally beautiful, these birds also possess a hint of that raw and savage glamour of which raptors are so imbued. There was to be no let up in today's performance; the shrike very kindly continued to indulge us. The shimmering heat and open scrubland was also reminiscent of more Mediterranean climes, which, if you try hard enough, can almost help you forget about the M25 and the drive home.

Of owls and raptors

Isle of Sheppey: owls, raptors and frozen feet

The approach of winter meant only one thing to us: wintering birds of prey. We therefore duly headed across the Thames to the Isle of Sheppey in north Kent. Although Sheppey (as we referred to it) can feel even more godforsaken than would Dungeness in the first days after the Apocalypse, it is an excellent place to see wintering raptors and owls. Our first birding encounter of note on this bleak and windswept isle occurred earlier in the season, when we happened upon a sighting that we were truly blessed to behold.

On a lone visit to the RSPB reserve at Elmley, and much to Panda's seething jealousy, I managed to locate a roosting Long-eared Owl in the orchard. Having learned of its presence courtesy of the information board, I scoured the dense and tangled thickets in a desperate bid to find the bird. After much fruitless scouring, after which I had come to the conclusion that the orchard was totally owl-less, I suddenly clapped eyes on a small fragment of rich-brown feathering that was only just visible through the tangled foliage. Yes! That had to be it! But I had to actually see the bird rather than simply a few square inches of its feathers. With all the stealth of a Special Forces sniper, I carefully slithered beneath the overhanging branches, inched myself up onto my knees, and then, ever so gently, raised my bins to my eyes. I was rewarded with great views of this magnificent bird glaring at me with its piercing orange eyes, its ear tufts fully erect as if bristling with irritation at such a brazen intrusion of its privacy. I savoured the view for as long as was polite and then carefully back-tracked in an attempt not to disturb the bird any more than I already had. I did feel a bit bad, though the owl didn't seem to mind too much and soon resumed its midday slumber. In addition to having obtained such good views of this bird, I also found one of its beautiful flight feathers; this was duly taken away and placed on my desk at work as a memento of the occasion. In retrospect, I acknowledge that it was quite irresponsible to have crept so close to a roosting owl, and I certainly wouldn't encourage others to do this. Though on a subsequent trip to Elmley with Panda, this beautiful creature was to prove that it was not quite as shy and retiring as it had initially led me to believe.

When I returned a week or so later with Panda to the exact same spot, the owl was nowhere to be seen. However, we soon became aware of the beckoning motions of another birder on the other side of the orchard. We rushed to join him, and were greeted with a view that sent our jaws dropping to the ground and our eyeballs straining at the sockets. Some 30 or so feet in front of us, and in full view, the owl was nestled on a branch right out in the open, dozing like a little plump and self-satisfied cat that didn't have a care in the world. This bird was clearly not quite the shrinking violet I had assumed it to be, and even the presence of a very noisy and extremely irritating child could not ruffle even one of those plush feathers. We could not believe our luck and looked on in wonder until the parts of our brains that process visual images were buzzing and crackling with a surging torrent of neurotransmitters. The owl was still present even after we had returned from the long trek out to the reserve and, knowing that such a cherished sight would likely not befall us again, we enjoyed this exquisite spectacle one more time.

It was also around this time that there was a Cattle Egret – quite a rarity – at Elmley; it was hanging around the cattle (as any self-respecting Cattle Egret would) on the rough grazing land. Much to Panda's annoyance, I saw the bird quite well on a lone trip there, though I subsequently returned with her in an effort to relocate it. Unfortunately, all we saw were the tips of its wings as it fluttered around in a cattle-churned furrow in the hazy middle distance. Naturally, Panda did the honourable thing and omitted it from her list of sightings, as you surely can't claim to have seen a bird if all you actually do see are the tips of its wings. And how could we be sure they were not the wings of a Little Egret – another white-coloured, though much commoner bird – or even, for that matter, an albino Curlew?

We also visited Elmley in the depths of winter, in the fervent hope of seeing Merlins and Peregrines and other such goodies. This time, our long walk out to the reserve was rewarded with the spectacular sight of a Short-eared Owl as it drifted menacingly into view, before swooping onto a fence-post and doing its best – though, I'm afraid, failing – to try and outdo the Long-eared Owl's brazen performance. On subsequent trips to Sheppey, we headed for the raptor viewpoint at Capel Fleet; on one occasion, acting on a tip-off, we also went to the coast, to Shellness and the Swale NNR.

Although the term 'nature reserve' conjures up images of nice warm visitor centres with cafés, there is certainly no such luxury on this bleak stretch of coast. Leysdown-on-Sea, which you have to pass through in order to get to the birding spots, is, in my view, the most dreary and depressing seaside town, though it hardly qualifies as a town, that I've ever had the misfortune to visit. It makes Canvey Island seem almost glamorous in comparison and makes Southend-on-Sea feel like Las Vegas. In the words of *The Smiths'* former frontman Morrissey, this really is "the coastal town that they forgot to close down".

Once clear of Leysdown, you suddenly discover that the road to Shellness is riddled with 10-foot-wide bomb craters, overflowing with muddy water that threaten to swallow your car whole. And if you actually reach the weather-beaten hamlet of Shellness with your car – and also your nerves – in one piece, you discover that it appears to be completely sealed off by a raised bank and low concrete wall, with accompanying *Keep out* signs that would make anyone who was not born and raised there feel about as welcome as a British soldier at a Taliban reunion. And then beyond that are the coastal marshes and rough grazing land, which are so bleak and desolate, and in winter so bone-chillingly cold, that even an Emperor Penguin that had just braved an Antarctic winter would think twice. Surely this place simply had to come up with the goods in order to make all these deprivations worthwhile.

As we rounded the hamlet and trudged along the shingle beach, we caught sight of a large silver bird flying low over the salt marsh beyond – it was a male Hen Harrier. We rushed ahead and then leapt up the tussocky bank to get a better view, but it was nowhere to be seen. In a bid to ease our bitter disappointment, a male Sparrowhawk rather obligingly performed a spectacular and dashing fly-past and then perched atop a fence-post just long enough for us to get the scope onto it. After a short but bitterly cold walk, and much to our relief, the male Hen Harrier returned; we enjoyed amazing views in the scope as it patrolled to and fro across the frozen wasteland in search of prey. As if this wasn't spectacular enough, out of nowhere a small dark bird suddenly burst forth and belted along in the wake of the harrier, twisting and turning like a mini fighter aircraft – a female Merlin. This was the bird we had come to this godforsaken place to see, and here it was in hot pursuit of the harrier, in the hope of picking off a panic-stricken bird put to flight by this marauding silver phantom. I had read of Merlins doing this on Sheppey, though I didn't think I'd be lucky enough to see it with my own eyes. What a sight! As swiftly as it appeared the Merlin was gone, though we continued to eagerly watch the Hen Harrier until it too disappeared into the frozen wastes beyond. In the dwindling winter daylight we headed back to the car, our near frostbitten fingers and toes surely a price worth paying.

On other trips to Sheppey that winter, at the raptor viewpoint at Capel Fleet, we saw the odd female Hen Harrier amid the deluge of Marsh Harriers, though they were nothing like as spectacular as the silver phantom at Shellness. We also saw quite a few Short-eared Owls, some of them bouncing around the skies seemingly for the sheer fun of it. Another of these owls was taking itself a little more seriously, patrolling low over the rough grassland in characteristic fashion; on one occasion we also got very good views of a Barn Owl doing likewise at dusk. But the most memorable bird to be seen at this location was still to come. As we disembarked from our car a cold winter's day, we had no idea of the treat that lay in store.

As we approached the viewpoint, I assumed that the huddled group of birders silhouetted against the sky were on one of the organised raptor-watching excursions I had read about – and very nearly booked myself and Panda onto. However, it soon became apparent that this was no organised trip; these birders had come from far and wide in the hope of seeing the Rough-legged Buzzard that had been reported as frequenting this spot. I was soon pointed in the direction of a bird, perched on a fence-post in the middle distance that was thought to be the 'Rough-legged', though nobody seemed to be certain. Its head was so pale it reminded me of a Red Kite, and every so often there was a tantalising glimpse of a bold white tail (a key diagnostic feature of this bird) as it fidgeted on its perch. One birder seemed to be quite happy that it was indeed a Rough-legged, though he was also careful to add that he was no expert. Another, who was clearly the expert and 'Alpha male' of the entourage, was a little more cautious and wanted to see it fly before he could be certain of its identity.

After what seemed like an eternity, and in the rapidly dwindling daylight, the bird finally lifted off from its perch and flew low and purposefully – presumably in the direction of its roost site. As it flew in a circuit across the backdrop of the prison and the bleakness beyond, all scopes – including mine – watched every move it made. I didn't have a clue what I was meant to be looking for, though as the bird finally made off into the distance, the Alpha male looked up from his scope and announced rather casually that he was happy that it was indeed a Rough-legged. Panda and I looked at each other in disbelief. Wow! Rough-legged Buzzard! As this raptor is a scarce winter visitor from more northerly latitudes it possesses a bleak and wintry glamour that makes it all the more special – a bit like a Snowy Owl or a Gyr Falcon, not that I have seen either of these birds. As I always do in such circumstances, I hastily sent my brother a text in order to inform him of the amazing bird that we had just seen and he hadn't! Don't feel too sorry for him though, as, when we fail to see bird, he announces he is dancing a jig to celebrate (though I think he stole this line from the TV comedy *Peep Show*, so he's not even original).

We returned to the raptor viewpoint a couple of weeks later, where we saw the same bird again. This time, as night was starting to descend, it again took off and flew in a circuit against the backdrop of the cold skies, which were positively aglow with vast swathes of yellow-tinged crimson from the rapidly retreating winter sun. As if it knew that this was the last we'd see of it, the bird rather obligingly decided to prolong its departure by pausing to hover every few moments, like a giant Kestrel. Against the glorious Technicolor of the winter skies, this was most definitely a sight to behold

Miscellaneous treats

That winter we also headed to Minsmere. Here we saw a small gang of Snow Buntings foraging on the windswept beach and a female Sparrowhawk flying back and forth across the reed-bed in front of the Bittern hide. Unfortunately, we did not manage to see any Bitterns, and so we also went to Lea Valley Park in Hertfordshire, "the best site in which to observe Bitterns in Britain" (Evans, 2001).

When we got to the Bittern watchpoint we were told that no Bitterns had been seen there for a couple of months – which was wonderful news! We needn't have worried though, as only a short walk from the watchpoint there was a small patch of reeds in which a Bittern had been reported as 'showing'. We raced along in an urgent bid to see the bird before it disappeared into the reeds, never to be seen again. Lady Luck was, however, on our side, and as we approached the small huddle of birders and curious onlookers, we were informed that it was indeed still showing. Although it was partially obscured by the reeds, we were able to get good views in the scope as it stood motionless with its head pointing skywards, doing its best – and very nearly succeeding – not to be seen. This was the first time I had seen a Bittern at such close quarters; my only other sightings had been brief glimpses of birds in flight at Minsmere. Panda was delighted as this was the first time she had ever seen a Bittern. This had also become something of a 'bogey bird' for her, after several trips to Minsmere and not a Bittern in sight.

Around this time we also headed for Rolls Farm on the Essex coast, which was almost a rival to the Isle of Sheppey in terms of bleakness. With the kind help of other, more seasoned, birders, we managed to see our first Slavonian Grebes, a Red-necked Grebe, Red-breasted Mergansers, Goldeneyes and a distant Great Northern Diver. We also saw a small flock of Brent Geese on the mudflats. The highlight for me, however, was the spectacular sight of a Peregrine as it dashed across the salt marsh in twisting aerial pursuit of a wader. Despite its best efforts to escape, the wader was no match for the Peregrine and was swiftly plucked out of the sky before it even had a chance. We felt sorry for the unfortunate wader but tried to remind ourselves that such is the cruelty of nature. Notwithstanding our genuine sorrow at the wader's demise, I felt sure that there could be few things to rival such a savage winter spectacle.

Optical debacles

"This is my rifle; there are many like it but this one is mine..." As a soldier is useless without his rifle, so is a birder without a decent set of optics. But bins and scope are not simply tools to be used in the pursuit of one's goal. They often become "the object of desire in a long relationship with optical technology; an affair that's central to most birders' lives and which borders on a marriage" (Cocker, 2001). Like a soldier's rifle, your bins and scope almost become an indispensable part of you as a birder. Although a good set of optics most certainly does not a good birder make, they can sometimes speak volumes – not only about your bank balance given the ridiculous price of optics these days – but, more importantly, about your birding calibre. The optics you wear around your neck and carry atop your tripod can sometimes – though by no means always – give others a pretty good idea of your level of interest and commitment. Some birders may become more obsessed with their optics than they are with the birds and birding, salivating over the top brands in much the same way that a fashion victim would over certain designer labels. Some, on the other hand, will care little about the brand name of their optics as long as they do the job. Others may even revel in inverted snobbery, proudly opting for the lesser-known – not to mention cheaper – brand names. Notwithstanding such personal idiosyncrasies, no self-respecting birder can deny the crucial importance of a good set of optics.

I no longer remember my very first pair of bins, though I recall getting a pair of Heron ones. I do remember my first scope though – a Bushnell Spacemaster. This was a damn good scope in those days and one that served me well throughout my early birding years; my brother still has his, though I have long since sold mine. When I recently got back into birding, I bought a pair of Bushnell bins for something like £40 via eBay. At the time I had assumed they were pretty good bins. But it didn't take me long to realise that if you want bins that don't mist up every time there's a spot of drizzle in the air, you have to fork out for a pair that are waterproof. Up until then I didn't even know there were such things as waterproof bins; how we must have suffered in the early years!

So I treated myself to a pair of Opticron bins for £220 and very pleased with myself I was too. It was also around this time that, given my burgeoning interest in birding, I treated myself to a Nikon spotting scope, which also came with a free tripod. Off I trotted with my new bins and scope, feeling very much the born-again birder. The honeymoon period with my new optics soon started to wear a bit thin though, and with the occasional snatched glimpse through better – and more expensive – optics, slowly but surely the limitations of my own bins and scope came sharply into focus…if you'll pardon the pun. I started to yearn for something just that little bit better. And then my obsessive streak started to kick in.

On Christmas Eve 2005, I went to Minsmere with Panda for a day's birding. While in the RSPB shop perusing the optics in the glass cabinet, I noticed a Nikon Spotting scope for around £225. It was both larger and – so I presumed – better than my existing model. When I peered through it with the zoom lens from my existing scope I was suitably impressed. Over the course of our day's birding, I convinced myself that an upgrade was very much in order. I justified this to my nagging conscience by appealing to its sense of altruism, and by offering it a deal: if I bought this new scope I would very kindly let Panda have my existing one, together with the tripod, completely free of charge. Despite her initial protestations that I should try and sell them instead, she eventually acquiesced. I handed over the money to the man in the shop and took charge of my new scope. My kindness to Panda was not limited to acts from which I would also benefit, and the next day – Christmas day – I presented her with her first pair of decent bins: some Viking bins that had set me back £150 (I would have spent more had I not already bought her loads of other presents). Panda was very pleased with her new bins. After a while, I most certainly was not.

Considering they were only £150 – compared with some that cost in excess of £1,000 – her bins seemed pretty good, hardly distinguishable from my own more expensive Opticrons. One day when we were out birding, I was having a peek through Panda's bins, whereupon I then made the mistake of switching immediately back to my own pair. I was struck with the sudden and horrible realisation that the field of view of Panda's bins was significantly wider than that of mine. Having now noticed this, every time I looked through my Opticrons it felt like looking through a couple of extremely narrow tubes; it was unbearable! I started to study all the figures, angles and measurements that one is bombarded with in the optical brochures and discovered that most Opticron bins tend to have quite a narrow field of view. I just couldn't bring myself to live with such visually restrictive bins after I had seen how the other half lived, even those with cheaper bins than my own. After much agonising, I eventually convinced myself that there was nothing else for it: I had to get some new bins. So off I trotted and treated myself to some top-of-the-range Opticron bins, worth in excess of £600. Ah yes, top-of-the-range bins, and this time with a wide field of view – success at last! Or so I thought…

Around this time I also started to have doubts about my new scope, which I had only purchased a few weeks earlier. When reading the 'small print', I realised that the scope was not in fact waterproof, but only water-resistant. I had wrongly – and very foolishly – assumed that all scopes would be waterproof simply because they are generally quite expensive pieces of kit. I was kicking myself for handing over so much money without informing myself fully of the product I was buying. In addition to my self-recrimination, there was now an urgent voice starting to echo in my neurotic mind: I *have* to get a better scope, one that is fully waterproof. So, having persuaded my brother to buy both my brand new scope and my old bins – the ones with the narrow field-of-view – I rushed out and bought a brand new Opticron scope, which also came with a free tripod, for just under £500. This time there was no messing about: the word 'waterproof' was fully emblazoned on the box for all to see. Surely this time there could be no doubt.

Soon after purchasing both the top-of-the-range Opticron bins and the fully waterproof Opticron scope... Yes, you've guessed it: I started to have more doubts. I was not happy with the optical quality of the bins. When I looked through them there sometimes appeared to be distortion towards the edge of the picture, i.e. as if you could see the spheres of the two concentric eyepieces down which you peer superimposed one upon the other. With regard to the scope, I was far more pleased with this than I was with the bins, though at higher magnifications (I had a zoom lens) I couldn't help noticing that there was considerable loss of clarity and darkening of the picture, especially in bad weather. I was also concerned that the rubber eyecup almost threatened to tear off every time I undid the stay-on case. After much agonising and soul-searching, I finally went back to the shop from which I purchased the bins and told the lady I was not happy with them. After I reluctantly agreed to try out virtually every other pair of bins in the shop, even ones in which I didn't have the slightest interest, she eventually relented and agreed to give me a refund. The money was, of course, duly spent on a new pair of bins, though this time I drove all the way to the RSPB shop at The Lodge, in Bedfordshire. I eventually settled on some top-of-the-range Nikon bins for just under £800, though only after rigorous and exhaustive field tests against some RSPB bins, plus also top-of-the-range Leica and Zeiss models. I didn't bother with the

Swarovski bins, as virtually every birder and their dog seemed to have a pair, plus I didn't really like the general look of them anyway. But what to do about the scope?

After lengthy negotiations with my conscience, and after offering it a deal it could not refuse, I eventually decided that I would, very kindly, give the scope to Panda as a gift. We would sell the Nikon scope that I had previously donated to her and would then spare no expense in purchasing the scope of my dreams. I therefore ordered a top-of-the-range Swarovski scope from a discount online retailer – a model I had previously tested at an Optics day at Minsmere (yes, we drove all the way to Minsmere from south Essex just to try out scopes!). When my new scope arrived, I fitted it atop my tripod and with much glee started to focus on random garden objects. However, my initial excitement slowly gave way to a nagging anxiety, as I noticed a distinct shimmering effect in the background of the picture. Try as I might to ignore it, I simply could not – not when I had spent over £1,000, in what was the culmination of a long series of optical crises. I made a telephone call to Swarovski, who assured me that there most definitely should not be any shimmering effect. I therefore packed up the scope and arranged for it to be returned to the retailer whence it came.

We then went back to Minsmere to conduct more field tests, this time specifically on a new Nikon field scope. Despite assurances to the contrary from staff over the telephone, the new zoom lens I wanted to try out with this scope was not in stock. It was vital that I test this particular lens, as I had read worrying news of it having a narrow field of view. In order to make up for having lured me all the way to Minsmere under false pretences, the staff in the shop advised me to visit the Viking Optical shop, which I was assured was just down the road. Once there I fully tested all the top scopes to my heart's content. The field of view on the new Nikon zoom lens was indeed too narrow for my liking, and I also didn't like the top Leica and Zeiss scopes either – mainly because of the dual focus wheels, which I found too fiddly. I was left with the Swarovski scope – the same model that I had previously bought and then returned due to the shimmering. Although there was no noticeable shimmering on the individual scope I tested on this occasion, I was still a bit dubious. Eventually, and very reluctantly, I returned home undecided and distinctly unsatisfied.

Yet I was determined I would not let indecision get the better of me, and, after more protracted agonising, decided there was only one thing for it. I headed to the RSPB shop at The Lodge one more time with the aim of buying a Swarovski scope, the same model I had previously bought online and then returned, which I would thoroughly put through its paces before parting with a single penny. Once at the shop, and with the scope firmly in my clasp, I stared through it like a man possessed for what seemed like an eternity – zooming in and out, focusing and re-focusing, until I had not only fully satisfied the maxim 'try before you buy', but had fully convinced myself that there was not the slightest trace of any shimmering effect. Then, and only then, did I dare to hand over my debit card.

Together with the zoom lens, the scope cost me the best part of £1,500. Although this left a gaping chasm in my bank account, it was surely money well spent, as it had the effect of finally putting an end to all these debacles – at least concerning scopes. Now all I needed to do was erase from my memory the time I subsequently succumbed to curiosity and looked through a pair of Swarovski bins. Like Saul on the road to Damascus, when I lifted these bins to my eyes the heavens opened and I saw clearly for the first time why every birder and his or her dog own a pair. Oh, and by the way, I later discovered that the shimmering effect on the Swarovski scope was down to heat haze in my garden and nothing to do with the actual scope at all!

In search of raptors – again

Operation Goshawk – phase 2

With the winter raptor season now at an end, our attention soon started to turn towards spring, and Goshawks. Early spring is the only time in which you are in with a fighting chance of finding this extremely elusive and secretive bird, and so, obscenely early one sunny day in April, we set off to Elveden forest, near Thetford, in the hope of seeing one of these magnificent creatures.

After trudging through the forest at Mayday Farm, and after hanging around for an hour or so at the spot I had frequented the previous year, we saw nothing that even came close to resembling a Goshawk. But we still had one more trick up our sleeves. Earlier in the day, we had asked a guy who appeared to be a forestry worker if he knew where the Goshawks were. He told us that we were in the wrong location and that all the twitchers, as he put it, went to another spot towards which he proceeded to direct us. In the late morning sunshine, Panda and I headed off to this area in the hope that we may be in with a chance. No sooner had we arrived than we made enquiries of another birder, who duly informed us that the Goshawks had indeed been showing that morning. Praying that we had not left it too late in the day (Goshawks are notorious early risers), we paced the three quarters of a mile or so through the forest as fast as was humanly possible (well, for us anyway) until we reached what remained of the huddle of birders. We set up the scope and waited.

Shortly after seeing an escaped Red-tailed Hawk soaring high over the forest, our attention was drawn to another raptor, this time soaring low over the coniferous treetops in the middle distance. In a flurry of activity I located the bird in my scope, following it in flight for all I was worth, while Panda watched it through her bins. As I had previously learned to my bitter disappointment, separating Goshawks from female Sparrowhawks is not always easy, and I nervously eyed the bird in a desperate bid to take note of its salient features while it was still in view; notable among these was its general bulky and heavy-chested appearance, and the conspicuous and somewhat bulging white undertail-coverts (feathers at the base of the tail, on the underside). As soon as the bird disappeared from view, and as faces were prised from the eyepieces of bins and scopes, all the birders present were in unanimous agreement: Goshawk. I couldn't believe what I was hearing. I had pretty much expected an inconclusive verdict, or the report of a probable Goshawk if we were lucky. But there was no doubt among the assembled birders, all of whom appeared to be far more authoritative than I. Finally I had seen the bird that had been eluding me for two years, and what is perhaps the most enigmatic and secretive of all the UK raptors. Panda and I grinned inanely at each other and almost broke into a little dance to celebrate. Goshawk! Yes! Right up there with the Rough-legged Buzzard on Sheppey! We left the forest with our heads held high and positively wallowed in the glory of our triumph all the way home.

A few weeks later we headed for the Forest of Dean in Gloucestershire and the raptor viewpoint at New Fancy – "perhaps the best site in Britain for seeing Northern Goshawk" (Evans, 2001). After a comfortable night in a Bed and Breakfast, followed by a lovely, if rather rushed, breakfast, we went straight to the viewpoint. There were no Goshawks, but we did see quite a few Crossbills at very close quarters as they clambered around in the pine trees immediately in front of us, since the viewpoint is elevated, affording birders a wonderful panorama across a sea of pines. We had seen Crossbills for the first time, if only very fleetingly, a few weeks before in Elveden Forest, while looking for Goshawks. But this was the first time we had seen them in full Technicolor as it were, and such dazzling close-up views of these beautiful birds had already made the trip worthwhile, even if the Goshawks decided not to show. We needn't have worried though, as we soon spotted a hawk soaring high over the treetops, which we and another birder were able to successfully identify as a Goshawk. Once I became familiar with the subtle differences between these birds and Sparrowhawks in the field (i.e. as opposed to in books) – for example the longer wings and lazier wing-beats – I felt a surge of confidence in my newfound identification skills, realising that I didn't always have to rely on other birders. We saw another Goshawk soon after this, but I only caught the briefest of glimpses as it plummeted into the treetops. Panda had seen it in a full and spectacular Peregrine-like stoop – probably part of its 'rollercoaster ride' display flight. Other views were more distant, and as morning became afternoon, and as it became clear that any self-respecting Goshawk would now be safely tucked away under the forest canopy, we packed up our things and headed off.

After another night in the Bed and Breakfast, we returned to the same spot early the next morning, though for some reason the Goshawks were nowhere to be seen. Maybe it was a bit breezy for them, as they seem to favour clear sunny skies with little or no wind. Having satisfied ourselves that we had given them sufficient time to put in an appearance, we headed off to Symonds Yat. Here, from the safety of a cliff-top RSPB viewpoint, Peregrines could be observed sitting on the nest. Upon arrival at the viewpoint, we learned that there was indeed a Peregrine on the nest, tucked away in a small crevice high in the rock face. There was a second Peregrine perched on a gnarled tree up on the cliff, as if on sentry duty, guarding the approach to the nest. As we were enjoying these birds in the scope, a flurry of excitement erupted among a couple of other birders present. A pair of Goshawks had just been spotted, and after being pointed in the right direction, I watched as one of these spectacular birds roved menacingly past the viewpoint directly in front of us – and much to the annoyance of the Peregrine on guard outside the nest. Then another Goshawk (or maybe it was the same one) came into view once again, only to slowly drift away and out of sight. Panda and I beamed with success and congratulated ourselves on having seen yet another of these awesome birds, this time much closer than at New Fancy.

As we descended from the viewpoint and headed back to the car, something began to trouble me. As I was looking at the second Goshawk through my bins, I had noticed an orangey-coloured barring to the upper chest. I checked in my field guides, which confirmed my worst suspicions: Goshawks do not have such colouration – but male Sparrowhawks do! I couldn't understand it, as the first of these birds certainly looked pretty big. The other birders also seemed pretty sure of themselves, one of them quite clearly affirming that the first bird was a definite Goshawk. Yet Panda informed me that she had overheard this very same birder mistaking a House Martin for a Swallow (or *vice versa*), and being corrected by his colleague. That was it: these birders were clearly not to be trusted; the only reasonable explanation was that we had just seen a pair of Sparrowhawks. Although a little disappointed, I had at least learnt a valuable lesson: be confident in your own identification skills, and don't assume that other birders know what they're talking about simply because they look and act – and talk – the part.

We ended our weekend in Gloucestershire on a high note with spectacular close-up views of Mandarins, including the more subtle though no less beautiful females. We also enjoyed a pair of Bullfinches hanging around the leafy garden of a hotel where we treated ourselves to a pot-of-tea-for-two in the fresh air of the late afternoon. As the next day was a bank holiday, and as we needed to bring ourselves gently back down to earth after the high of our weekend, we thought we would head for Weeting Heath in a bid to see the resident Stone Curlews. Despite the horrendous heat haze, we did manage to locate one of these goggle-eyed weirdoes as it sat motionless with its characteristic fixed stare and had fantastic views through the scope due to its close proximity. Our next port of call was Wayland Wood, where we thought we'd chance our arm with the local Golden Pheasants. After doing a thorough circuit of this small wood, the closest we had come to seeing one of these birds was hearing a few muffled shrieks from the depths of the tangled undergrowth. These calls may well have emanated from a common Pheasant that was just trying to taunt us and anyway, I had no idea of the respective differences, if any, between the calls of these two species. Feeling somewhat deflated, we returned to the car. What confronted us there really sent our spirits crashing.

One of the car's back windows was completely smashed, and glass fragments littered the back seat and the ground adjacent to the car; it had been well and truly broken into. Whoever did this had made off with Panda's digital camera, worth nearly £400, which was full of photos taken during our weekend in Gloucestershire, including close-up shots of those Mandarins. They had also taken my overnight bag, which contained personal items such as clothes, toiletries, medication, books and also my beloved *Father Ted* DVD box set. Needless to say we were both extremely upset. Panda was devastated at the loss of her treasured camera, not least because she had yet to download all the photos from our weekend away. We felt a deep sense of our property and personal privacy having been violated in the most uncaring and callous manner, plus a seething anger towards whoever had perpetrated this heartless act. I knew from my experience of working in the criminal justice system that, even if by some miracle the perpetrator(s) were caught and convicted, the sentence imposed would likely be so lenient that it would be a deep insult to both of us, especially if they were juveniles (for both adults and juveniles alike, a community sentence would probably be a strong likelihood). I was also concerned about how I would continue with my job as Youth Offending Team officer, which entailed supervising the type of amoral individuals who perpetrate such affronts to all that is good and decent.

Norfolk summer raptors revisited

Although Panda's car being broken into was very upsetting, we were eventually able to put it behind us, and as spring turned to summer, our thoughts inevitably turned towards Honey

Buzzards and Montagu's Harriers.

Our first attempt to see Honey Buzzards was a total disaster from start to finish. Having left early in the morning – for Great Ryburgh in Norfolk – we were no more than ten minutes or so down the road when Panda's car started to overheat dangerously. We waited patiently for the AA to arrive, and when they finally did, we were advised that the problem appeared to be due to a leak in the water tank's cap. Much to our relief, he also said that, as long as we replaced the cap, there was no reason why we couldn't proceed onwards to Norfolk. Luckily we were on the edge of a large retail park. After a short wait for the Ford parts shop to open, we bought a new cap, screwed it on nice and tight and much to our relief were soon on our way once again. Shortly after this, and now on the M25, the car started to overheat again. We pulled over onto the hard shoulder and summoned the AA – again. This time we were told it could be the head gasket and were duly towed home – after first being taken to the wrong town. Although Panda's car would need to be taken to a garage first thing on Monday, we decided that if we didn't hang around too much, we could still make it to Norfolk in my car. So off we set once again.

Eventually we arrived at Great Ryburgh, still early enough – we hoped – to be in with a chance of seeing a Honey Buzzard. At least on this occasion we had had the foresight to bring some garden chairs with us and duly took up position in the sweltering heat among the other birders. It was unbearably hot; there wasn't even the slightest hint of a merciful summer breeze. Nothing stirred in the blistering midday sun and the bright blue skies were cloudless and still. I overheard one birder saying that, contrary to popular belief, this was not good weather for Honey Buzzards, as although they needed thermals on which to soar, there also needed to be at least some movement of wind in the air. It appeared that, on a day like this, any self-respecting Honey Buzzard would be seeking refuge from the baking sun. Slowly but surely, it became clear that we were certainly not going to see any 'Honeys' today, and hence decided to cut our losses and head home, putting it all down to a bad day.

On our next attempt, we arrived nice and early in the morning, after an overnight stop at a rather lovely Bed and Breakfast in the nearby village of Swanton Novers. The weather was noticeably more temperate than on our previous attempt, and we hoped that luck would be on our side. Not long after our arrival, we were watching the skies around the treetops when a large bird came into view; it duly started to wheel and soar in characteristic raptor-like fashion. In all likelihood it was either a Common Buzzard or Marsh Harrier, though when I looked through the scope I did notice that it had a distinctive and strangely familiar silhouette. I knew exactly where I had seen this silhouette before: pictures in field guides of Honey Buzzards in flight. Simultaneously, and in his fine southern Scottish accent, the birder next to us calmly but authoritatively announced, "That's a Honey, that's a Honey." I couldn't believe what I was hearing. As if the bird knew that, given its rarity, it had revealed itself for quite long enough, it duly disappeared into the blue skies. To add substance to his assertion, the Scottish birder pointed out the bird's distinctively small and pigeon-like head. When I rather neurotically questioned him as to whether it was a 'definite Honey', he answered without hesitation and in the affirmative. We had finally seen the bird that had been eluding us all this time, and for even longer than had Goshawks – until we eventually caught up with them. Honey Buzzards are rarer than Goshawks, perhaps not quite so elusive, though every bit as sought after. As we had done with our first Goshawk, Panda and I grinned inanely at each other and breathed a long sigh of relief. Yes – finally! Honey Buzzard!

As well as helping us catch up with our first Honey Buzzard, the Scottish birder also very kindly gave us precise directions to the Montagu's Harrier nest site – such information being a closely guarded secret within the public domain, for obvious reasons. Flushed with success and eager to 'kill two birds with one stone', we bid Great Ryburgh and our Scottish friend a fond farewell, and headed off along the country roads that meandered through the sprawling Norfolk countryside.

Once at the Monty's nest site, we set up our scopes and cast our gazes expectantly across the vast arable field before us. Other birders at the site informed us that the female had been showing; the female would be great, though a male was the ultimate prize. We were not to be disappointed, as after only a few minutes, the male came sweeping across the field in all its silver majesty. Its sumptuous plumage was resplendent in the morning sunshine, and the finer diagnostic features – such as the black wingbars – were clearly visible. We had wonderfully intimate views as it patrolled to and fro across the field. At one point it even rather obligingly perched on a low hedge, sitting there in the sunshine for all to gaze longingly upon. Great as the show was, nothing could prepare us for the final encore, which was to be a real showstopper.

After a brief absence, the male was spotted flying low across the field. Then the dark brown female – out of sight until now – came into view, flying eagerly towards the approaching male, as if to greet him. As they neared one another, the female manoeuvred into position, almost turning upside down in mid-air. At this point the male correspondingly pulled sharply upwards, and then effortlessly dropped a parcel of food into the waiting talons of the female. A split second later the manoeuvre was complete; the male continued on his way, while the female dropped down into the nest and out of sight. We couldn't believe what we had just seen. To see a Montagu's Harrier – perhaps the UK's rarest breeding raptor – is a privilege in itself. To get such great views of a silver male in the scope, complete with black wingbars and other diagnostic features, is something else altogether. To witness a mid-air food pass over the nest, and in crystal-clear close-up through one's scope, is surely a blessed experience. To witness all of this on the same morning that you proudly see your first Honey Buzzard – probably the UK's second rarest breeding raptor – is surely to stretch and distort the superlatives to the point that they become meaningless – especially for Panda, for whom both birds were firsts. With our pupils still dilated and our auras positively aglow, Panda and I congratulated ourselves on what was perhaps our most successful morning's birding ever, not to mention an experience that will take its rightful place alongside our most cherished birding memories. Although we were both still walking on clouds, as it was nearing lunchtime there seemed to be only one way of celebrating. So we duly headed off to the café at RSPB Titchwell and ordered two teas and two toasted Stilton and mushroom baguettes. It would surely have been rude not to.

Capercaillies – they don't exist!

What shall we do for our holiday this year? We could go to the Scillies, or even the Shetlands. Chasing after rarities is all well and good, but I'm not sure I want to spend my whole holiday doing it. Plus, we'd be pretty much dependent upon other birders to tell us what we are looking at – not much fun, and could even be quite stressful which kind of defeats the idea of having a holiday. Hold on a minute, I still haven't seen birds such as Crested Tit, Capercaillie, Black Grouse, Dotterel and Osprey. Panda still hasn't seen Ptarmigan, and Golden and White-tailed Eagle, plus it's been years since I've seen any of these birds myself. It would also be nice to see things like Red Squirrel, possibly even Pine Marten! Also, I haven't been to Scotland for years, and it would be nice to see those mountains and rocky coasts again. Panda has never even been to the Highlands – she would love it there!

So we booked ourselves onto an organised birding holiday based in Strathspey, a mere stone's throw from the foot of the Cairngorms. Our holiday, carefully selected from a mouth-watering array in the brochure, was chosen to maximise our chances of seeing all the Scottish specialities, particularly the eagles. We would search the Abernethy Forest for Crested Tit and Capercaillie, spend a day on the Cairngorm plateau looking for Dotterel and Ptarmigan, and also head for the Isle of Mull, on the west coast, in search of both Golden and White-tailed Eagle. We couldn't wait!

After one of the most hideous weeks I have ever experienced at work – where the task of ensuring all the loose ends were fully tied up seemed like a never-ending quagmire of anxiety and stress – I was finally able to pull myself away from my desk and start focusing on the birding extravaganza that lay ahead. As I worked in a Youth Offending Team the last thing I wanted was to be halfway to Scotland and suddenly realise I'd forgotten to do something really important – something that could potentially mean one of the little 'ASBO enthusiasts' I supervised would hang themselves in custody, and it would be my fault. I can just see the newspaper headlines now.

The bedroom window of our hotel looked directly across to the beautiful Cairngorm Mountains, and the summer air was so fresh you could almost taste it. We were so far north it barely got dark at night, and every morning we were serenaded by a band of piping Oystercatchers from the field outside our bedroom. We also saw an early-morning Roe Deer in this field. It was truly beautiful, a world away from the concrete, noise and rush hour traffic we had left behind.

No sooner had we arrived at the hotel than we explored the local river in search of Dippers. Although there was no sign of any little brown birds with white bibs, we did see plenty of Grey Wagtails; okay so they're not exactly rare, but as well as being a new bird for Panda, it had been years since I'd laid eyes on one of these delightful birds.

We started the first day in style, with a female Black Grouse and her chicks seen from the minibus and a briefly glimpsed Tawny Owl as it made off into the stunted roadside forest. We saw male Black Grouse on the distant slopes of Tulloch Moor and a juvenile Goldeneye, which was somewhat closer to hand on a small lake. (I have since come to learn, courtesy of one of our guides – a proverbial fount of local knowledge – that it appears there is some controversy as to whether this area is, in fact, Kincardine Moor as opposed to Tulloch Moor.) In Abernethy Forest we finally managed to catch up with a couple of very obliging Crested Tits. Contrary to our natural instincts to keep quiet lest our quarry should take flight, we were informed that 'Cresties' were actually attracted to human voices. Like the Pied Piper of the birding world, the same guide duly strolled along the road, while intermittently calling out "come on Crestie, come on Crestie". No sooner had he done so than a couple of these endearing little creatures appeared at the head of the column – no doubt curious as to what all the noise was about – and started to flit around in the roadside pines, right under our noses. Despite the fact that these birds don't keep still, making your average Blue Tit seem almost sluggish, we had some excellent views through our bins as they scurried around in the trees like Goldcrests on cocaine. On a lonely highland loch we saw distant Black-throated Divers in their resplendent, chequered summer plumage, an even more distant Red Grouse and then, much to our joy, a not-so-distant Osprey.

The Osprey is one of those birds that I should really have caught up with by now, on passage migration (when a bird passes through a certain area on its migration route) – but I just never seemed to be in the right place at the right time. In recent years I drove all the way to Rutland Water in Leicestershire, the site of an Osprey reintroduction programme, in a bid to see one of these birds – but alas I failed. Much as I would have loved to catch up with an Osprey on 'passage' or at Rutland Water, there was a certain sense of purity in seeing one against its native backdrop of a tranquil Scottish loch. Needless to say, Panda and I relished the site of this magnificent bird as it patrolled across the waters in search of a meal, and duly congratulated ourselves on another new sighting. We were to see plenty more Ospreys as the week unfolded, including on the nest at Loch Garten where we also saw a chick being fed.

One particular day was dedicated to seeing Dotterel and Ptarmigan high on the Cairngorm plateau. After alighting from the minibus, we commenced a steep uphill trudge, the like of which I had not experienced since my long-abandoned hillwalking days. Shortly after setting off from the car park, one of the guides spotted a couple of Twite by the side of the track – a species that I had never seen before. I think I actually saw the birds in question but couldn't be certain as there were Meadow Pipits at every turn, perched seemingly on every boulder and on every fence-post along the track. Panda managed to see the Twite and delighted in reminding me that she now had 'one up on me'.

As we climbed steadily higher into the chill air, the valley below gradually fell away beneath us, and the steep track gave way to a series of even steeper rocky slopes. We eventually reached Coire Cas – an armchair-shaped corrie ringed with steep, precipitous walls – whereupon our guide's keen ears detected the call of a Snow Bunting. We continued to ascend the steep slope adjacent to the corrie, though the top of this slope eventually proved, much to our disappointment, to be a cruelly deceptive false summit. Onwards and upwards we continued. The promise of the plateau – and rest – seemed like the proverbial pot of gold at the end of the rainbow. It felt like an eternity before the gradient finally started to ease beneath our aching lower limbs. Meanwhile, and unlike we mere mortals, our guide simultaneously shouldered his scope and tripod and was able to ascend the steep rocky slopes with all the skill and grace of a mountain goat.

Soon we were rewarded with the sight of a male Snow Bunting, perched proudly on a rock for all to see. Not only was this fine bird in full breeding plumage, it also had fledglings in tow. We also saw hen Ptarmigan scattered about, almost perfectly camouflaged among the mottled rocks. When we looked closer through the scope, it became apparent that at least one of them had chicks. Ptarmigan was a definite first for Panda. It was also no less of a joy for me, as it had been many years since I had seen these birds high on the slopes of Ben Nevis and Glencoe.

Having finally reached the relative mercy of the vast Cairngorm plateau, our next quarry, the Dotterel, was proving to be a much trickier target. After scouring the high slopes all around, and after walking quite a bit further across undulating, boulder-strewn terrain, we were almost ready to admit defeat. Our guide went off ahead to see whether it would be worth pushing on further, onto even higher ground, while we took a well-earned rest. During this time, I spotted a lone Reindeer trotting across the summer snows below us. We had seen Reindeer being herded on the lower slopes earlier in the day, not far from the car park, though to see a lone animal high on the plateau felt much more 'real' and gave the sighting a genuine air of wilderness authenticity. Shortly after the guide returned, and as we were in the process of trying to convince our unwilling limbs that it was worth making a final push, he suddenly spotted a Dotterel just ahead of us – it had been there all along! It trotted around for a good few seconds, affording us a brief glimpse of its reddish underparts, plus the characteristic V-shaped stripe on the back of its head. The prospect of missing out on Dotterel after such a long and hard climb was unthinkable, and we duly congratulated ourselves on our last-minute success, not to mention on having seen another new bird.

Although we thought the worst was over, the descent from the plateau proved to be even more gruelling than the climb up. When we finally made it to the car park, my leg muscles were actually shaking and part of me wanted to collapse in a physically spent heap on the floor. Yet there was one last bird to see: a stunning male Ring Ouzel, perched on a fence. We made a quick dash for it, managing to snatch a brief glimpse in the scope before it made off (this was a bird that I had previously ticked years before, but could not actually remember seeing). En route to a much-needed tea stop, we saw another Red Grouse. As we sat by the tranquil waters of Loch Morlich, proudly surveying the mighty hills from which we had just descended, a beautiful Red-throated Diver in summer plumage drifted effortlessly past in the afternoon sunshine. This was indeed a perfect antidote to the day's mountain rigours, as were the soothing bottles of stout that, once back at the hotel, we felt we had thoroughly deserved.

The Findhorn Valley was also the target of our birding endeavours. In the lower part of the valley we saw Stonechat, Dipper and also caught glimpses of Peregrine and Merlin. On our way to the upper valley, we were treated to a spectacular display by two Ospreys as they flew in close proximity to the minibus, almost seeming to follow us. Then, as if waiting until its audience was in prime position, one of these birds started to hover, and, with wings pulled back and talons pushed forward, it suddenly dropped out of the sky, plummeting vertically down towards the winding river and out of sight. A few moments later it re-emerged, victorious, with a fish in its talons, and continued its flight up the valley, stooping its head every so often to take a nibble from its slippery prize.

In the spectacularly beautiful upper Findhorn Valley, we saw a Peregrine soaring majestically across the wide-open valley, as if proudly surveying its vast territory. We saw both Feral Goats and Red Deer aplenty, including stags silhouetted high on the ridges above, in classic *Monarch of the Glen* pose. We saw a female Ring Ouzel jumping around amid the jumbled boulders at the head of the valley, and, thanks to our guide's razor-sharp eyes, a Mountain Hare grazing on the grassy plains in its greyish-brown summer coat. Alas there was no sign of our main quarry, Golden Eagle, though thankfully we had already seen two distant birds earlier in the week; the distant views were partly compensated by the antics of a very courageous Merlin, who proceeded to mob the eagles in true Kamikaze fashion.

An early morning visit to a private estate failed to secure even the merest hint of the much sought-after Capercaillie, though the guides assured us that they had plenty more tricks up their sleeves. Slavonian Grebes in their breeding plumage were seen at Loch Ruthven RSPB reserve, and a distant male Hen Harrier soared majestically across the hilltops. An evening jaunt around the loch that, earlier in the week, had provided our first Osprey, afforded us further views of Black-throated Diver in their chequered black and white finery and a lone Whooper Swan (I think the divers also had chicks with them, though I certainly didn't see any). On this twilight jaunt we also saw a Red Grouse with chicks scurrying along the road in front of the minibus, and a Woodcock on its 'roding' flight rounded off the evening nicely.

Our holiday was progressing well. Roe Deer were encountered throughout the week and we also saw Sika Deer and plenty more Red Deer. Back at the hotel, the bird feeders were swarming with Siskins, and much to our delight a lone Red Squirrel scurried about among the pine trees right above our heads. Common Hares were encountered frequently; to our growing holiday list we also added Red-breasted Merganser, Goosander, Golden Plover, Raven, Cuckoo, more Dippers,

Redpoll (or is that Lesser Redpoll?), Crossbill, Wheatear, Whinchat, Mistle Thrush, Treecreeper, Swallow, Great Spotted Woodpecker and seemingly endless Spotted Flycatchers and Common Sandpipers. Although Mull and the promise of eagles still lay in store, we were starting to become concerned that we had not yet been able to snatch a glimpse of a Capercaillie; a nice strutting male was what we really wanted, though a dour female would suffice. We had passed many 'Capper woods' on our travels – the only thing missing were the Cappers themselves! Slowly but surely it started to dawn on us that this was going to be the 'bogey bird' of the holiday, but the guides assured us that there would still be another opportunity to try and catch up with it.

Early next morning, we headed for the Isle of Mull in search of eagles. Still in the minibus, we looked on as beautiful Scotland passed us by. Upon reaching Fort William, we craned our necks to catch a glimpse of the spectacular north face of Ben Nevis. Although I was a naive and idealistic teenager when I had first cast my eyes upon these mighty cliffs, in the intervening years this grandiose and primeval landscape had lost none of its powers to inspire awe and wonderment. I wished that we could stop to admire the high chiselled cliffs skirted by their summer snows, though on this occasion a brief glimpse through the minibus window would have to suffice. We soon reached the Corran ferry crossing, where I briefly glimpsed a Black Guillemot. Regrettably Panda missed it, but she needn't have worried, as we soon saw another one from the ferry crossing to Mull. This was a new bird for Panda and the only other 'Black Guill' that I had seen was some ten years before.

Once on Mull, we headed to an exposed spot on the coast, where we happened upon a small crowd of birders. We were soon pointed in the direction of a couple of White-tailed Eagles on a small rocky island close inshore. They were sitting motionless, like enormous stone statues, or else like guards on sentry duty at the gates to their watery kingdom. It had been nearly 20 years since I had been lucky enough to see one of these birds on the Isle of Skye. The sight of these magnificent creatures was every bit as exciting as that first memorable encounter. As the eagles did not seem to be going anywhere in a hurry, I left Panda gazing in wonder through the scope and nipped round to the other side of the headland for a quick toilet stop. Before I had finished, I saw a huge bird flying high and purposefully over the sea and against the spectacular backdrop of the large rocky island beyond. I hurriedly made myself decent and raised my bins to my eyes. With its enormous rectangular wings and relatively small head and tail, there was no question as to its identity: it was another White-tailed Eagle. Feeling very proud of myself, both for spotting and also successfully identifying it, I rushed back to the others to share my news. Before I could open my mouth, Panda informed me that, while I was gone, one of the eagles she was watching had taken flight in my direction, and that, unfortunately, I had missed the spectacle. I reassured her that I had just seen the bird as it flew past out to sea, and that it was indeed a sight to behold. As we watched Arctic Skuas passing out to sea, what appeared to be the very same eagle – having flown a short circuit of the headland – now came back into view, landing in a tree on the horizon. As time was now short, we were only able to gaze through the scopes very briefly before continuing around the island.

Sometime after bidding farewell to the eagles, another of these enormous beasts stopped us in our tracks as it flew over the minibus. It was carrying a large piece of carrion – something like half a sheep! No sooner had it appeared than it was gone, though we were consoled by a couple of Common Scoters fairly close inshore. It was nice to see these birds relatively up close and personal for a change, rather than as grubby black dots a mile or so off the north Norfolk coast. Although further eagle sightings were hampered by the encroaching weather, the skies did clear up a little after lunch, and we managed to see Hooded Crow, moulting Red-breasted Mergansers, Snipe, Rock Pipit and Kittiwake. We had also seen Common Seal, Shag and a raft of moulting Eiders earlier in the day. Our day on Mull had been fantastic, but our sojourn was now, and much to our disappointment, rapidly drawing to a close.

Just as we were about to depart, a last-minute Golden Eagle put in an appearance high above an adjacent ridge. I leapt off the minibus and hastily set up my scope. Despite the eagle's best efforts at distraction, discussion among the others on board had now turned to the need for haste in order to make the imminent ferry crossing. We were given the option of getting a later crossing, but unfortunately Panda and I were outvoted in what can only be described as a landslide defeat. Democracy had spoken, and just as I was about to feast my eyes on the 'Goldie' that I had now located in my scope, I was forced to acquiesce to the majority vote and climb aboard the minibus. Although we were not too happy at having to tear ourselves away from it, we had to admit that we had had a great day. As we reluctantly bid farewell to Mull – a truly beautiful isle – we reassured ourselves that sometime, hopefully in the not too distant future, we would return.

Our holiday was now rapidly nearing its end. It would not, however, be complete without clapping eyes on a Capper. So we headed to another private estate, which we proceeded to circumnavigate in the minibus at ultra-slow speed. As it passed by outside our window, the forest was scoured by eager eyes in the hope that we would see something stirring. There was nothing – not even the slightest hint of movement amid the trees or on the forest floor. I hoped that our fortunes had taken a turn when we encountered some Capper dung and a small downy feather on the bank next to the track, and also when, soon after this, we saw a group of birders huddled by the side of the track. We pressed on, but still saw nothing; with every passing minute and with every square inch of Capper-less forest that we passed by, I knew our luck was gradually running out. I was right: all that we encountered in the forest was an oppressive stillness and an all-pervading lack of Cappers. I even got to the stage where I was examining every tree stump and broken branch in the last desperate hope that it might – just might – turn out to be something vaguely resembling a Capper. By the time we completed our circuit we had still not seen the merest hint of even the slightest movement within the forest, let alone any sign of a bloody great big grouse! Our guide blamed disturbance caused by the group of birders for our failure. By now I no longer cared. I had a throbbing headache from endless rubbernecking; I was even starting to wonder if Cappers actually existed.

Our last port of call was Chanonry Point on the Moray Firth, a prime site for catching up with Bottle-nosed Dolphin. While waiting patiently for these creatures to put in an appearance, we saw Guillemots, Razorbills and Grey Seals out in the harbour, the latter also coming in close to shore. We also saw passing Kittiwakes, Common Terns, and a single Shag, Fulmar and Arctic Tern. Don't ask me how our guide knew it was an Arctic as opposed to a Common Tern, but he certainly knew his stuff.

As if conscious that a crowd had now gathered, at the appointed hour the dolphins duly performed for the waiting onlookers. In twos and threes they would swim close to the shore at the point where the two perpendicular beaches meet and where the land is said to slope off steeply into deeper water. They would leap up to reveal their dorsal fins and dark shiny backs. With the exception of a couple of 'possibles' years ago in Wales, way out in Cardigan Bay and which may even have been Harbour Porpoises, I had never before seen wild dolphins. The performance, right under our very noses, was truly a sight to behold and every bit as exciting as any of the birds we had seen. Once we had had our fill of the dolphins we moved on to Munlochy Bay in the hope of seeing some now fairly scarce farmland birds. There was no sign of any Tree Sparrows, though we did happen upon a Yellowhammer atop a telegraph pole singing for its supper: "a-little-bit-of-bread-and-nooo-cheese". A Red Kite – no doubt part of the local reintroduction scheme – also graced us with a fly-past.

The last day of our holiday was almost over. On the way back to the hotel, we made one last stop at some 'Capper woods'. However, no matter how quiet we were, and no matter which way we turned, all we heard was silence, and all we saw were trees. Our guide even pointed out a tree stump, upon which a male Capper had once put on a lekking display for previous holidaymakers. But it was not to be – nothing stirred and the tree stump remained bare. Despite our guide's valiant last-minute efforts, the Cappers had finally defeated us, and Panda and I returned to the minibus convinced that, like the Loch Ness Monster, Cappers do not actually exist. It seems that our failure to connect with any Cappers at all on this holiday was down to that most unpredictable and fickle of mistresses: Lady Luck.

A twitch too far

After the success of our holiday in Scotland, we were itching for some more action. Unfortunately, we couldn't afford another holiday of this type for at least another year, but we could a week in Norfolk. So in the third week of October, still within the autumn migration season, we headed once again to the place where our relationship was forged – a place that had almost become our spiritual, and most certainly our birding home, the north Norfolk coast. We had toyed with the idea of going to the Scillies, but firstly couldn't afford it and, secondly, we really didn't relish the idea of spending all week doing nothing but chasing after rarities, most of which we wouldn't have a hope of identifying for ourselves. A less than enjoyable brush with the twitching fraternity at the end of our holiday would confirm that we had made the right decision.

Once in Norfolk our first port of call was Titchwell, where there had been a report of a Whiskered Tern – a bona fide rarity. Upon reaching the lagoons, we were informed that it was last seen about an hour ago, since when it had long since disappeared over yonder. So we sought solace in the hides, where I did my best to feign interest in the usual cast of waders and wildfowl. The Brent Geese were quite a spectacle though, especially when I paused to consider that they had likely just flown all the way from some far-flung frozen wasteland in the Arctic Circle. I used to turn my nose up at geese, but now they are among my favourite birds. There is something really evocative about these hardy global travellers, and there is surely no finer sight than skeins of honking geese filling the reddened twilight skies, or pirouetting earthwards in turn, landing en-masse in a grassy field, or skidding to a halt upon the crowded surface of a winter lake.

Titchwell is always a nice place to visit anyway, even if there is nothing much around; we could always have a look around the shop and then treat ourselves to the obligatory Stilton and mushroom baguette at the café. Before we did so, we thought we'd have one last look to see if the Whiskered Tern had reappeared, as the birders on the footpath seemed to be looking at something. Upon joining them, we were told that the tern had indeed been relocated, and we raised our bins to our eyes as it flew elegantly towards us. It was a beautiful mottled juvenile bird, and it flew within ten or so feet of us as it scoured the perimeter of the lagoon in search of fish. It seemed completely oblivious to the long line of birders watching its every move. It would fly to the top of the lagoon, then skirt its perimeter adjacent to the path from where countless eager eyes stared in wonder to then return to the top of the lagoon and start this circuit over again. At times this delightful little bird was so close that I didn't even bother with my bins, whilst every so often it would plunge gracefully into the water to pluck out an unsuspecting morsel.

As we were overdosing on this exquisite spectacle, Panda suddenly let out a cry of "Water Rail!" I hastily raised my bins to see one tip-toeing nervously along the edge of the lagoon to find cover amid the overhanging vegetation. Panda was very pleased with herself for having both spotted and identified this bird by herself, all within the blink of an eye. The Water Rail was a new bird for Panda. It was also quite a treat for me, as I had only ever seen this very secretive and elusive bird on one previous occasion, which was over 20 years earlier. We also saw a Ruff on the lagoon. This was courtesy of 'Clarkey', a birding friend from the early years who we had happened upon at Titchwell. The Ruff was another new bird for Panda, one that I had not seen for some years. So as to toast a very successful first morning, we went first to the shop and then to the café to place our orders.

Later that day we drove eastwards across Norfolk to the raptor roost viewpoint at Stubb Mill, "the best place in the country to see Cranes in winter and Norfolk's leading site to see Merlin, Hen and Marsh Harriers" (Glenn, 2006). The viewpoint overlooked a large expanse of open grassland and scrub; in terms of bleakness this area was more than a match for the Isle of Sheppey in Kent. However, unlike the places we frequented on Sheppey, this site was very isolated, and as the winter darkness of early evening was fast approaching, we felt quite vulnerable. We half expected to be approached by some crazed serial killer with thick-rimmed glasses and a nervous twitch on the lookout for new victims. Marsh Harriers started to gather in the encroaching gloom, though impressive as these birds were, we were primarily interested in the Cranes.

Shortly after we arrived another car pulled up. Its occupant got out and started to approach us. We were quite relieved when we realised he had not come to kill us but was an Norfolk Wildlife Trust volunteer who planned to count the Cranes as they came in to roost. He asked us to move our car back to the small car park down the track. Despite my protestations that I should go with her, Panda insisted that she go while I stayed and waited for the Cranes. As Panda was walking back to the viewpoint, to my delight and also my horror, a handful of Cranes appeared out of nowhere in the murky skies and started to descend towards the dense grassland below. I couldn't bear the thought of Panda missing them and ran down to the start of the track to see if I could see her. She was only a few hundred yards away, and I frantically beckoned her to hurry. But, alas, she did not make it in time. Although technically I had seen the birds, the joy of a new sighting was ruined by the fact that Panda had missed it altogether. Just as we were lamenting Panda's misfortune, another 30 or so Cranes appeared in the last throes of daylight. This time they were closer and, despite the fact that the skies were rapidly darkening, we were even able to catch a quick flash of black, red and white as they flew effortlessly across the vast openness beyond. With their long wings, protruding necks and outstretched legs, they resembled flying crosses as they drifted steadily lower, gradually losing height until they eventually disappeared into the darkness below. We grinned at each other, congratulating ourselves on another successful sighting, not to mention a thoroughly successful day: wonderful views of Whiskered Tern, plus also Water Rail, Ruff and now Crane. Four new birds for Panda and two for myself – not bad for a day's birding! We trudged back to the car in darkness, periodically looking over our shoulders to check for Jeffrey Dahmer look-alikes. When we eventually reached the car we breathed a sigh of relief on seeing that it had not been broken into, and eagerly returned to Wells-next-the-Sea and the comfort and safety of our Bed and Breakfast.

Another destination we visited was Flitcham Abbey farm, near Sandringham, "probably the best place in Norfolk to see Little Owl" (Glenn, 2006). We returned here on at least another two occasions throughout the week. Despite spending literally hours in the hide at all times of the day, there was not the merest sign of anything even remotely owl-like. The skeins of honking Pink-footed Geese passing by on the wintry horizon were, however, a sight to behold, as were the flocks feeding on the hilltop fields, among which there was also a lone Barnacle Goose. A female Sparrowhawk swooped through the trees, a Buzzard patrolled over the fields and a pair of Egyptian Geese waddled around rather awkwardly in the foreground, their distinctive plumage bearing more than a passing resemblance to the make-up of a circus clown. We also saw our first Yellow-legged Gull; this is not exactly a rare bird, but it was all the more satisfying as I identified it all by myself with a little help from my field guide.

We also went to Holkham Hall in the hope of catching up with roosting Tawny Owls. Although being in possession of precise details as to the very tree in question, even down to the part of the tree favoured by the owls, and despite scouring every inch of branch and pine needle with much prolonged rubbernecking, there was again not the slightest hint of anything resembling an owl. We also tried to catch up with Tawny Owls in the vicinity of our Bed and Breakfast in Wells-next-the-Sea. Virtually every night we were serenaded by hooting Tawny Owls that sounded so close we could reach out and grab them. Needless to say, any attempts to locate these owls during daylight hours ended in failure.

Across the road at Holkham Pines we tried in vain to locate a Yellow-browed Warbler that had been reported there. I had clearly not learnt my lesson after the last time we had tried – and failed – to see one of these birds here. I still hadn't the faintest idea what their call sounded like, and so it's hardly surprising that, amid the endless stands of pines, we didn't realistically have a hope in hell. But we did manage to see some rather endearing Goldcrests at close quarters and watched intently as they performed their agile acrobatics upon the thinnest of twigs. Holkham Pines is a lovely place; it is always worth a visit, if only to gaze upon the massed ranks of Pink-footed Geese that invade the grassy fields in large numbers every winter. We stared in wonder as endless skeins descended from the skies – with their characteristic high pitched calls echoing far and wide – to join the flocks of roving grazers below. This was a wonder of the natural world that we felt truly blessed to behold.

We were still determined not to let the Yellow-browed Warbler get the better of us, and so headed off to Holme, where one had been reported hanging around the observatory. Rather ironically, we were almost entirely dependent upon my brother, in East London, to inform us – courtesy of the Internet – what birds were around on our own doorstep in Norfolk. We got tantalisingly close to the bird this time, even locating the exact tree in which it had been seen flitting about only a few minutes previously. Despite noting much avian activity in this tree, which was far from straightforward amid the wind-ruffled leaves, every bird had either totally disappeared in the split-second that it took to raise our bins to our eyes, or else when one did keep still for more than a nanosecond, it proved to be either a Goldcrest, Chiffchaff or Willow Warbler. As some birders, when they are not sure if they've seen a Common or Arctic Tern, refer to 'Comic Tern', should these birds therefore be referred to as 'Wiffwaffs' or 'Charblers'? Hmm, I think not. We had one more go at catching up with the Yellow-browed Warbler later in the week at Titchwell; it was no use, and we missed out on this bird yet again.

At Holme Bird Observatory, we were invited to watch some birds being ringed, and as neither of us had seen this before, we duly accepted. We watched intently as a Redwing, a female Blackcap, a rather unfortunate and mangy Blue Tit and a couple of tiny Goldcrests were put through their paces. The birds were removed from the small duffle bags inside which they had just been wriggling for all they were worth, shoved head-first into some kind of plastic case to be weighed, and then manhandled while their vital statistics were taken. After the rings had been clamped around their delicate legs, the birds were finally granted their freedom. I have to say that neither Panda nor I found this a pleasant experience; I struggled to justify to myself why these birds should be put through such an uncomfortable and stressful ordeal, presumably in order simply to satisfy our scientific curiosity. If linked directly to a programme of conservation or species protection, then I can see that in such circumstances maybe the ends justify the means. In the absence of such a direct link, I struggle to see why any animals should be subjected to such treatment. I believe passionately in wildlife conservation, though also believe even more in treating animals with respect, dignity and compassion.

At Cley, we managed to catch up with the White-rumped Sandpipers that had been reported there. Although a new bird for both of us, not to mention being a rarity to boot, I did not find this sighting especially enjoyable. I was almost completely dependent upon other birders, both in locating the birds and, once located, in correctly identifying them. Left to my own devices, I would no doubt have mistaken these inconspicuous and distant sandpipers for either Dunlin or Little Stint...had I even noticed them in the first place. On the way back from the hides, a Cetti's Warbler, deeply hidden from view, was doing its best to entice us with its explosive and colourful song. True to form with such a notorious 'skulker', any attempts to see it proved fruitless. This was doubly painful for me; not only had I yet to see a Cetti's Warbler, but Panda had snatched a glimpse of one earlier in the week that I had failed to see.

Thanks to my brother and his laptop back in London, we also managed to catch up with a Pectoral Sandpiper and a Pallas's Warbler at Salthouse. Both of these birds are rarities, and both were firsts for Panda and me. I was glad to finally catch up with a 'Pec' as I had recently failed to see one, having come tantalisingly close. We had excellent, if brief, views through the scope, including of the characteristic white braces and pointed breast pattern; the latter feature is, as I understand, where the bird derives its name. Unfortunately, we could not hang around to enjoy the 'Pec' as much as we'd have liked to, as we still needed to locate the Pallas's Warbler. After a short but brisk walk to a tangled grassy knoll, adjacent to and on the landward side of the beach, we joined the long line of birders patiently awaiting the reappearance of the Pallas's. We were not to be disappointed, as after only a few minutes the bird duly reappeared. As well as performing spectacularly and at close quarters for the assembled birders, this little gem was far more brilliant and colourful than could possibly have been imagined from a quick glance at the illustration in the field guides. It also had no hesitation in showing off its main diagnostic features, namely its yellow central-crown stripe and yellow rump. I positively revelled in being able to note such features for myself, especially after the run-around we had been given by the Yellow-browed Warbler at Holme. I was also tired of being more or less dependent upon more experienced birders to confirm the identity of the rarities that I saw. This time I didn't need other birders – just me and my field guide.

Exquisite though this bejewelled little bird was, nothing could beat the spectacle of the dashing male Merlin that tore across the lagoon back at Titchwell, in pursuit of a small bird fleeing for its life. As well as being an inherently impressive and awe-inspiring bird, I also identified this bird all by myself – and identifying falcons in flight is not always straightforward. Despite hearing a shout of "Hobby" from another birder who looked like a 'top boy', I stuck to my guns and went with my gut instinct that this was indeed a Merlin. My previous sightings of this incredible bird, with its distinctive manic flight and tight, rapid wing-beats, informed me that I was right. A quick perusal of the falcons in my field guides also confirmed the decision. The quick flash of bluish-grey upperparts as it twisted in mid-air after its quarry indicated that it was a male. I approached the top boy (who was not in fact a top boy after all, but merely doing a good impression) and he acceded to my better judgement. Yes, it was a Merlin. Not a new bird, but a great encounter nonetheless, and inducing a warm glow of satisfaction that I had correctly identified it.

I experienced a similar feeling in the hide a while later, when another birder thought he had found a rare wader. As excitement started to spread throughout the hide, I had the unfortunate responsibility of informing everybody that it was in fact a Knot. Admittedly it was my field guide that clinched the decision, but it was nevertheless also informed by my gut feeling that this was a very Knot-like bird and not at all like any kind of sandpiper, which is what certain people were starting to talk of. This incident also served as my own personal redemption from my 'Murray moment' at Titchwell a year earlier.

With regard to our decision not to go to the Scillies, we felt somewhat vindicated when, on the way home from our week in Norfolk, we stopped off in Suffolk to see a Red-flanked Bluetail, another very rare bird indeed. Although we both eventually managed to get good views it…and a very beautiful bird it was too, it was generally not a very enjoyable experience. This was due to the behaviour of other birders, some of whom were – and unusually for birders – rather rude, selfish and inconsiderate, to say the least.

Upon arrival there was the usual small crowd and feverish activity, together with a handful of blokes with enormous camera lenses and serious expressions. Thanks to the help of a fellow birder, I quickly caught a few fleeting glimpses of the bird before it flew off. Panda did not manage to see it, and there followed a frantic 45 minutes or so in which the small crowd desperately tried to relocate the bird in the thick scrub. Despite being very elusive, Panda did eventually see it.

In their desperation to see the bird, some people stood directly in front of Panda, who is only 5ft 3" tall, thus obscuring her view and clearly not caring whether she saw it or not. In his haste to move in front of her, one birder knocked past my telescope and tripod and would likely have knocked it over had the tripod legs been extended further. Another person barged past Panda, knocking the rucksack full of camera equipment from her shoulder; he did not apologise or even seem to notice her. Some birders – most notably the camera-toting 'long lens brigade' – were trying to get too close to the bird, likely frightening it and causing it to retreat deeper into the scrub; this would also potentially add to the already considerable stress that such a vagrant would already be under. Despite the area being a conservation site, certain people had little or no respect for this habitat and were trampling over the vegetation in their desperate attempts to see the bird. This could clearly lead to the locals – who had already had their picturesque village invaded by hordes of cars – feeling even greater antagonism towards birders.

With the exception of a few friendly and helpful individuals, the atmosphere at this 'twitch' did not generally feel very positive. What I love about birding is that you meet such friendly people, and one of its joys is the shared experience of the special, the exciting, the rare and the elusive, and helping others to observe birds that one has just been privileged to see one's self. Having spent a week in Norfolk, frequenting such lovely places as Titchwell, Holme and Holkham Pines and exchanging pleasantries with people who simply enjoy watching birds and no doubt just being in such beautiful places, the atmosphere at this twitch could not have contrasted more. Apart from a few of the birders, the majority did not seem particularly interested in interacting with others; they did not seem to care about anything other than 'getting' the bird for themselves, whether it was a better view – even though others had yet to see it – or that 'all-important' photograph.

Once we had both seen the bird, and once Panda had calmed down (she was fuming), we left for Minsmere and, once there, made a beeline for the café. As well as enjoying, in the true spirit of *Withnail and I*, some much-needed 'cake and tea', we reminded ourselves that the simple pleasure of seeing birds is what it's all about. Bring on the Robins and Chaffinches!

Bibliography

BirdGuides Ltd. (2004). *The DVD-ROM Guide to British Birds* (Version 8).

Cocker M. (2002). *Birders – Tales of a Tribe*, Vintage.

Cocker M. & Mabey R. (2005). *Birds Britannica*, Chatto & Windus. Quote on114-115pp

Evans L.G.R. (2001). *Finding Birds in Britain*, BirdGuides.

Glenn N. (2006). *Best Birdwatching Sites in Norfolk*, Buckingham Press Ltd.

Mullarney K., Svensson L., Zetterstrom D. & Grant P.J. (2001). *Collins Bird Guide – The Most Complete Field Guide to the Birds of Britain and Europe*, Harper Collins.

Oddie B. (1983). *Bill Oddie's Gone Birding*, Methuen.

Oddie B. (1980). *Bill Oddie'sLittle Black Bird Book*, Methuen.

Robinson B. (1989). *Withnail and I: The Original Screenplay*, Bloomsbury.

Other natural history books by Brambleby Books

Arrivals and Rivals – A duel for the winning bird
Adrian Riley
ISBN 9780954334796

UK500: Birding in the fast lane
James Hanlon
ISBN 9780954334789

Feathers and Eggshells – A bird journal of a young London girl
Natalie Lawrence
ISBN 9780954334772

British and Irish Butterflies
Adrian Riley
ISBN 9780955392801

The Wild Flowers of the Isle of Purbeck
Edward Pratt
ISBN 9780955392849

Garden Photo Shoot – A Photographer's Year-book of Garden Wildlife
John Thurlbourn
ISBN 9780955392832

What's in your Garden – A book for young explorers
Colin Spedding
ISBN 9780955392818